100 GREATEST PITCHERS

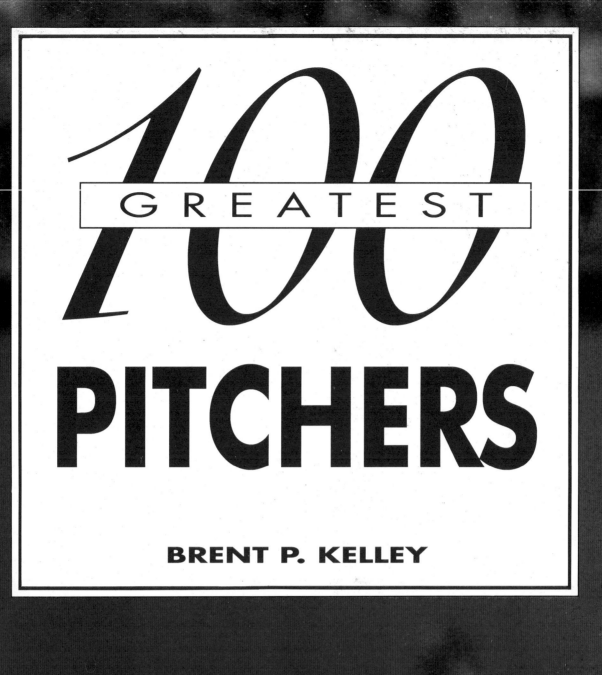

100
GREATEST
PITCHERS

BRENT P. KELLEY

BARNES & NOBLE BOOKS

PREFACE

This was originally written some years ago as a book of opinion, and it still is. Opinions change, however, and the emergence of new, young pitchers and the loss of form or early retirement of some of the older ones makes the list of men included here a constantly changing one. In the last decade no Cy Youngs or Sandy Koufaxes, or even Jim Palmers or Whitey Fords, have appeared on the scene. Years from now, though, we may well see Greg Maddux or Randy Johnson ranked up there with the elite of the pitching world.

This book includes my personal nominations for the best 100 pitchers of the twentieth century. My choices are based strictly on what these players did when they did it, not, for example, on what Joe McGinnity *might* have done in 1970 or what Roger Clemens *could* have done in 1910.

There are pitchers not included here whom some may feel belong. Roy Face is alluded to often in these pages, but he isn't here. Hippo Vaughn and Earl Whitehill and several other excellent pitchers are also not here. And, of course, some who were here in the first incarnation have now been bumped, outstanding pitchers such as Virgil Trucks and Freddie Fitzsimmons to name a couple.

The title, though, is *100 Greatest Pitchers*, not 106 or 111 or some other number. Maybe you, the reader, do not agree with my selections, and that's great. That's what being a baseball fan is all about.

At the end of the book, I have ranked these 100 men in the order I think they belong: the top 100 pitchers of the twentieth century from number one down to number one hundred. Even if you agree with my 100 choices, I know you won't agree with my rankings. You're welcome to try your own. It's hard to do.

I wonder how the Top 100 will look in another eight or ten years.

Brent P Kelley

This edition published by
Barnes & Noble, Inc.,
by arrangement with Brompton Books Corporation.

Produced by Brompton Books Corporation
15 Sherwood Place
Greenwich, CT 06830

ISBN 0-7607-0064-8

Printed in China

Revised and updated 1996

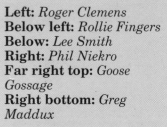

Left: *Roger Clemens*
Below left: *Rollie Fingers*
Below: *Lee Smith*
Right: *Phil Niekro*
Far right top: *Goose Gossage*
Right bottom: *Greg Maddux*

Previous page (clockwise from top): *Don Sutton; Walter Johnson; Don Newcombe (c) with Gil Hodges (l) and Roy Campanella; Catfish Hunter; and Tommy John with Tommy Lasorda.*

Page 1: *Lefty Grove*
Pages 2-3: *Nolan Ryan works on his 5000th strikeout in 1989.*

Grover 'Pete' Alexander

Grover Cleveland Alexander

Pete Alexander broke into baseball with a bang. His 28 wins for the 1911 Phillies is still the rookie record.

And that was just the beginning. Alexander dominated the National League for his first seven years. He won 190 games, including 30 or more for three straight years. He lost only 89, and he tossed 61 shutouts, including the single-season record of 16 in 1916.

But somewhere along the line he met an adversary stronger and more unrelenting than any batter he ever faced: the bottle. Although he went on to win 20 games three more times (for a total of nine times), and to tie Christy Mathewson for third on the victories list, with 373, the Grover Alexander from 1918 through 1930 was not a Hall of Fame pitcher.

Yet he had one last unforgettable moment of glory. He had been picked up by the Cardinals early in 1926 (at age 39) as pennant insurance. That year in the World Series he hurled two complete victorious games against the Yankees, and he saved the deciding seventh game by striking out the great Tony Lazzeri, second only to Babe Ruth in RBIs that season, with the bases loaded. And at the age of 40 'Old Pete' won 21 games.

The Alexander of 1927 may not have been the Alexander of 1911-17. But no one else was, either.

Above: *Grover Alexander set the rookie record for wins with 28 for the Phillies in 1911.*

Below: *Alexander with Cardinals manager Bill McKechnie. Alexander led the Cards to their first World Championship in 1926.*

Chief Bender

Charles Albert Bender

In the first decade and a half of this century Connie Mack and his Philadelphia Athletics had some of the greatest pitching staffs in history. At one time or another in this era, As moundsmen included such as Eddie Plank, Rube Waddell, Jack Coombs, Bob Shawkey and Herb Pennock, but the pitcher Mack wanted on the hill in the important games was Chief Bender. Chief, a full-blooded Indian, joined the As in 1903, straight from the campus of the Carlisle Indian School. Only 19 then, he was an immediate success, winning 17 games and having more innings (270) and more complete games (29) than he would ever have again.

He remained with Philadelphia for 12 seasons, winning 191 games for them with a .652 winning percentage. He was frequently used in relief, and 23 of his victories came in this role.

Mack's teams were the dominant force in the American League in the early teens, with four pennants in five years. The Chief pitched nine complete games in 10 Series starts, winning six and losing four.

In 16 full seasons, Bender won 210 games, with a 2.46 ERA.

Bert Blyleven

Rik Aalbert Blyleven

For nearly two decades Bert Blyleven was one of the premier pitchers in the game. He ended his 22-year career with 287 victories and almost 5000 innings, but was generally a well-kept secret over the years.

Born in Holland in 1951, he pitched 19 of his years in small media centers (Minnesota, Texas, Pittsburgh, Cleveland), and about the only times national attention was focused on him was when things didn't go well – like in 1986, when he gave up more home runs than any pitcher ever had, and 1980, when he was disqualified for two weeks over philosophical differences with Pirate management.

But he was a 20-game winner in 1973 and struck out more than 200 batters in eight different seasons; his career total of 3701 strikeouts is the third highest in history. He was a rarity among pitchers of his time, regularly finishing what he started; he retired with 242 complete games. His 60 shutouts are ninth most in history, and only two pitchers, Walter Johnson and Pete Alexander, in the entire history of baseball pitched more 1-0 games. And during his career (1970-92) he was generally acknowledged as having the best curve in the game.

Left: *Bert Blyleven pitched for the Rangers, Indians, Pirates, Twins, and Angels.*

Tommy Bridges

Thomas Jefferson Davis Bridges

Left: *Detroit pitcher Tommy Bridges warms up in the bullpen. The Tiger curveballer won two complete games in the 1935 World Series.*

Run down the list of the pitchers in the Hall of Fame. How many Detroit Tigers do you come across? In the book you are now reading there are nine pitchers who spent all or a major part of their careers in Tigertown, plus two others who had a few good seasons there. Only Hal Newhouser is in Cooperstown.

Tommy Bridges was the leader of the Tiger pitching staff for the decade of the 1930s. These were good times for good Tiger teams, for they featured players such as Hank Greenberg, Charlie Gehringer, Schoolboy Rowe, Rudy York, Eldon Auker and Mickey Cochrane. And curveballer Tommy Bridges took full advantage of the support he was given.

Tommy won 20 games three straight years (1934-36), leading the league with 23 the last year. As was the case with so many talented ballplayers, the war interrupted his career and prevented him from reaching the 200-win plateau, but he did reach a highly respectable total of 194.

Twice the American League strikeout leader, Bridges was on four Tiger pennant-winning teams. Tommy went 4-1 in post-season play and was the pitching hero of the 1935 World Championship effort, with two complete games and a 2-0 record.

Three Finger Brown

Mordecai Peter Centennial Brown

The first baseball dynasty of the twentieth century belonged to the Chicago Cubs. From 1904 through 1911 the Cubs won four pennants, including two World Series, and were second three times and third once. In those eight years they won 807 games, including 116 in 1906, still the all-time single season high.

Those Cub teams had an overabundance of top pitchers, including Ed Reulbach, Jack Pfiester, Orval Overall, King Cole and Carl Lundgren – all except Lundgren 20-game winners. But the ace of the staff for those eight years was Mordecai Brown, who was the chief rival of Christy Mathewson for the title of best National League pitcher of the early 1900s.

Called 'Three Finger' because of a childhood accident that cut off parts of two fingers, he used this disability to develop one of the game's most wicked curves. He won 20 or more games in a season six times (25-plus four times) and is easily one of the all-time great control pitchers, allowing only 1.9 walks per nine innings.

His career ERA is 2.06, third best in history, and he won 239 games on his way to the Hall of Fame.

Left: *Three fingers were apparently more of a help than a hindrance for Mordecai Brown, for he possessed a rare and dangerous curveball. He helped the Cubs win four pennants from 1904-11, and his showdowns with rival pitcher Christy Mathewson of the Giants were always a big thrill for fans.*

Page 12, top: *Fastballer Jim Bunning rears back for the Phillies.*

Page 12, bottom: *Bunning unleashes another mighty pitch. He won 19 games four seasons, accomplished 100 wins in both major leagues and by his retirement in 1971 had struck out 2855 batters, second only to Walter Johnson at the time.*

Jim Bunning

James Paul David Bunning

It's hard to believe that anyone could be critical of a man who won 224 games in a 17-year career and who is one of the few pitchers in history to win 100 games in each major league. But it's this criticism that kept Jim Bunning out of the Hall of Fame for so long. The problem: He won 20 games only once. That was in 1957, in his first full season in the majors.

True, he won 20 only once, but he spent his career with teams (Detroit, Philadelphia, Pittsburgh, Los Angeles) that, with two exceptions, were decidedly average, generally struggling just below the first division and a few points one side or the other of .500.

But he won 19 games in a season on four occasions, the most seasons anyone ever accomplished that. And he pitched two no-hitters – one in each league, one of only two pitchers to accomplish this in the twentieth century, and one of those was perfect.

Possessing a blazing fastball and excellent control, Bunning struck out over 200 batters in six seasons and led the American League twice and the National League once. He retired after the 1971 season with 2855 whiffs. At that time he was second on the all-time list, behind only Walter Johnson.

And, finally, in 1996 he was elected to the Hall of Fame.

Lew Burdette

Selva Lewis Burdette

The 1957 World Series: the Milwaukee Braves – their first; the New York Yankees – their umpteenth. Lew Burdette had been a good pitcher for several years, but he had pitched in the shadow of the great Warren Spahn. In this October in 1957 Burdette finally stepped out of the shadow. He became the first pitcher in 11 years to win three games and the first in 37 years to win three as a starter. Three complete games, two of them shutouts.

The 24-year-old Burdette was acquired, along with $50,000, by the then Boston Braves late in the 1951 season in exchange for Johnny Sain. He was 26 by the time he had made much contribution to the Braves' cause, but he eventually became the number two man on the staff and was a 20-game winner twice and a 19-game winner twice. In 10-plus seasons in Milwaukee he won 173 games, and at one time or another he led the league in most of the major departments: wins, ERA, percentage, innings, shutouts, starts, complete games.

The opposition might hit the ball off of Lew (they got more hits than he had innings in his career), but he won the games (203), and that's what counts in the end.

Left: *The Milwaukee Braves' Lew Burdette won three complete games against the Yankees in the 1957 World Series.*

Page 14: *'Actions speak louder than words' was never more true in the case of Philadelphia southpaw Steve Carlton.*

Steve 'Lefty' Carlton

Stephen Norman Carlton

The first four-time winner of the Cy Young Award, Lefty's thoughts and opinions about the game may forever remain a mystery. Unhappy with the media for alleged misquotes and made-up quotes, he stopped talking to them. When his long-time catcher, friend and confidant, Tim McCarver, retired and went into the announcers' booth, Carlton even stopped talking to him. Truly a man of principles.

Possibly the greatest year ever experienced by a pitcher was Carlton's season of 1972. Acquired from the Cardinals in spring training for Rick Wise, Steve became the pitching staff for the Phillies, a truly bad team. He went 27-10, with a 1.97 ERA, 30 complete games and 310 strikeouts. In each of these categories he led the league. His winning percentage was .730, a figure he would top twice in years to come.

The 1972 Phillies had a record of 59-97, with a team ERA of 3.66. Not counting Carlton, they were 32-87, with an ERA of 4.23. He had 20 more wins than the next winningest hurler on the team.

Carlton, who retired during the 1988 season, won 20 or more games in a season six times. His career win total (329) is second only to that of Warren Spahn among southpaws. In the strikeout department his record (4136) is second only to that of Nolan Ryan. Come to think of it, he really doesn't have to say anything to anybody to make his point. He was elected to the Hall of Fame in 1994.

Jack 'Happy Jack' Chesbro

John David Dwight Chesbro

One of the first to master the spitball, Happy Jack Chesbro pitched much larger than his 5'9" frame suggested.

His season of 1904 is, of course, legend: 41 wins, 48 complete games, 454 innings. But alas, that year ended on a sour note. His wild pitch on the last day of the season cost the Highlanders (Yankees) the pennant.

But Chesbro did much more than pitch one spectacular season. In a career that consisted of only nine full seasons, plus parts of two others, he won 198 games. He won over 20 games per season in four other seasons, and he is one of only two pitchers in history – the other is Gaylord Perry – to lead both leagues in victories. (He had won 28 for the 1902 Pirates.) He is the *only* pitcher ever to lead both leagues in winning percentage (1901 and 1902 in the NL; 1904 in the AL).

A neck injury in 1907 seriously curtailed his effectiveness, and this led to arm trouble, which in turn led to a 20-loss season in 1908. He retired before the 1909 season ended.

Eddie Cicotte

Edward Victor Cicotte

Since this book is concerned only with pitching ability, Eddie Cicotte must be given a prominent place on our list. Unfortunately, if our criteria had been based on moral values, the story would have been different.

One of the first knuckleballers, Cicotte spent his first nine years in the big time as a good number two or three starter for the Red Sox and the White Sox. He won over 15 games only once in this period (18 in 1913). But in 1917, at the age of 33, he blossomed, and over the next four years he ascended to the upper echelon of American League hurlers, winning a total of 90 games.

Both in 1917 and 1919 he led the league in victories, with 28 and 29, respectively. It was in that infamous latter season that he pitched the White Sox into the World Series and into the greatest scandal in baseball history.

In 1920 he added 21 wins, but then the 'Black Sox' scandal – the rigging of the Series – broke, and late in the season he and seven of his teammates were barred from baseball for life for their varying degrees of complicity in the fix.

Above: *White Sox knuckleballer Eddie Cicotte recorded 208 wins, including 28 wins in 1917 and 29 in 1919, in his scandal-shortened career.*

Top: *1904 was Jack Chesbro's finest year. He won 41 games that season, including 14 consecutive wins.*

One reason given for Cicotte's involvement was that he was 35 years old in 1919, and he knew that his days in baseball were numbered. Since he had no personal savings, the temptation of the money was just too great. If so, it's still no excuse. But the fact remains that Eddie left behind him a truly impressive record: 208 wins in slightly over 13 seasons.

Roger 'Rocket' Clemens

William Roger Clemens

The dominant pitcher in the American League during the late 1980s and early 1990s was Roger Clemens, the big Red Sox righthander. Spending only parts of two seasons in the minor leagues, he joined the Bosox in 1984 and by 1986 was the best pitcher in the game.

That year he won the first of his three Cy Young awards by going 24-4 with a 2.48 ERA as he led his team to the World Series. He was also named the AL's MVP. He followed in 1987 with another 20-win season and another Cy Young Award.

Through 1995, Clemens won four ERA titles and led the league in shutouts five times and strikeouts twice, including a major league record 20 in one game on two occasions. He has averaged nearly 8.5 strikeouts per nine innings for his career.

He spent some time on the disabled list in early 1995, but by mid-season he was back in the rotation and showing flashes of his old form. Now in his mid-30s, he has 192 wins through 1996 and has an excellent chance at 200 before he's through. At peak form, there has rarely been a pitcher who could approach Clemens' ability.

Wilbur Cooper

Wilbur Arley Cooper

Quick: Who holds the Pittsburgh Pirates' record for career victories? Without the name above as a hint, that could be one tough question. But then, questions about good men who played for weak teams are always tough.

This thin southpaw won 202 of his 216 victories for the Pirates between 1912 and 1924. He won 20 or more games per season four times, another Pirate record. And it could easily have been six, for he won 19 each in 1918 and 1919, both seasons shortened by World War I. Other team records he holds are most complete games (263) and lowest ERA (1.87 in 1916).

A good control pitcher who never struck out many batters, he toiled for mostly mediocre teams while in the Steel City. The 1917 edition was especially bad (51-103), but Cooper had perhaps his best record (17-11), when the quality of his support is considered.

He was never fortunate enough to pitch for a pennant winner, but the fact that he didn't do so in 1925 must have been especially galling. At the end of the 1924 season the Pirates sent their best pitcher (Cooper), their regular first baseman (Charlie Grimm) and their regular second baseman (Rabbit Maranville) to the Cubs for a journeyman pitcher (Vic Aldridge), a second baseman who wound up playing first (George Grantham) and a minor leaguer (Al Niehaus). On paper this trade should have made Chicago a contender; they finished last: The Pirates were the World Champions.

Above and below left: *Red Sox ace righthander Roger Clemens has won the Cy Young Award three times – 1986, 1987, and 1991. Clemens has led the AL in wins, ERA, strikeouts and shutouts using his 95-mph fastball and outstanding control.*

Right: *Pittsburgh Pirate Wilbur Cooper demonstrates his pitching form. Cooper set several team records, including four 20-plus win seasons, most complete games (263) and lowest ERA (1.87 in 1916).*

Stan Coveleski

Stanley Anthony Coveleski

Growing up in turn-of-the-century Pennsylvania and watching their dad work in the coal mines caused the Kowalewski boys to look elsewhere for a means of making a living. Changing the family name to Coveleski, four of these brothers turned to baseball. Frank pitched in the outlaw Union League, John was a minor league infielder-outfielder and Harry won 20 games three times in succession for the Tigers in the mid-teens. But the pick of the litter was baby brother Stan.

Brought up to the Athletics at the end of the 1912 season, he pitched well, but not well enough. He returned to the minors for another three years and learned to throw the spitball in 1915, while with Portland, of the Pacific Coast League. Cleveland brought him back up the next year, at age 27, and he became their ace for the next nine seasons.

He won from 22 to 24 games for them from 1918 through 1921, and he was the Indians' hero in the 1920 World Series with the Dodgers, winning three games, with an ERA of 0.67. Given to the Senators for two nonentities after the 1924 season, he had his fifth 20-win season in 1925 and led Washington to their second straight pennant.

His career consisted of 11 full seasons and parts of three others. He retired with 215 victories and a .602 winning percentage.

Above: *Spitball hurler Stan Covaleski.*

Right: *Covaleski achieved five 20-win seasons during his career.*

Above right: *The Baltimore Orioles' Mike Cuellar.*

Below right: *Detroit Tiger Hooks Dauss.*

Mike Cuellar

Miguel Santana Cuellar

On 4 December 1968 the Houston Astros sent three players to the Baltimore Orioles and got two in return. One of the three the Orioles received was a 31-year-old lefthander coming off an 8-11 season for the last-place Astros. What the Orioles really received was domination of the American League East Division.

Mike Cuellar was 29 when he finally made it to the majors to stay. He had been a pretty good pitcher for a pretty bad Houston team until the trade to Baltimore. There he teamed with Dave McNally, Jim Palmer and, later, Pat Dobson to form one of the top rotations of the twentieth century.

Cueller was the staff leader, winning 125 games over the next six years, five of which saw the Orioles win their division and three times make it to the World Series. He won over 20 games per season four times, the last time in 1974, when he was 37 years old.

He shared the Cy Young Award with Denny McLain in 1969, and he led the league in victories (24) in 1970. In 11 full seasons and portions of four others he won 185 games. Some trade.

Hooks Dauss

George August Dauss

George Dauss never did anything in a spectacular manner. Of average size and looks, he also threw a baseball in a fairly ordinary fashion, possessing a good, but not great, curve and an average fastball. Some say he threw a spitter.

But from the time he joined the Tigers, at the tail-end of 1912, until 1924, when he began working out of the bullpen, he took his turn in the rotation every four or five days, using his ordinary pitches to achieve very unordinary results.

His first 20-game season (actually he won 24 games) was his fourth, and he had 20-game seasons every four years for 15 seasons until his retirement, all in Detroit flannels. In all those seasons he never led the league in any major category, and doubtless that is why he has been so easy for many people to overlook.

Yet he was a remarkably consistent performer during a mediocre period in Tiger history. He finished his career in 1926 as one of the early relief specialists (11-4 out of the bullpen, with nine saves). No Tiger pitcher before or since has ever topped his 221 wins.

Dizzy Dean

Jay Hanna Dean

Baseball probably lends itself more to colorful characters than do other sports because the spotlight can rest longer on one man at a time – a batter's mighty swing, a great fielding play, a pitcher on the mound. And Dean was nothing if not colorful. A huge ego, with the talent to back it up, plus a small boy's outlook on life and an irrepressable sense of humor, these were the ingredients that made up Dizzy Dean.

From his rookie year with the Cardinals, 1932, until Earl Averill's line drive broke his toe in the 1937 All-Star game, there were few who could equal his pitching of a baseball. He won 20 or more games per season for four straight years, topped by 30 in 1934 – the last National Leaguer to reach that mark – and he led the league in strikeouts during his first four years.

After his injury he insisted on coming back too soon. In compensating for his toe, he injured his arm, and the blazing fastball was gone, and with it his greatness. He held on for a few years relying on breaking pitches and guts, but in mid-1941 he hung up his uniform to embark on a new career, one tailor-made for his special knowledge and engaging personality. Thus it was that he became one of America's favorite play-by-play baseball announcers on what today we fondly remember as 'old time radio.'

Above left: *Dizzy Dean, lively personality and ace pitcher for the St Louis Cardinals' Gashouse Gang, went 30-7 in 1934 and also had 195 strikeouts, seven shutouts and 24 complete games.*

Below left: *Dizzy, shown here with brother Paul 'Daffy' Dean, had a career winning percentage of .644 and was named to baseball's Hall of Fame in 1953.*

Right: *Unsung hero Paul Derringer was often in the shadow of fellow pitchers, despite shining performances. However, Derringer came out ahead in the end, winning 223 games in all.*

Paul 'Duke,' 'Oom Paul' Derringer

Paul Derringer

Paul Derringer rarely got the credit he deserved during his career. He pitched for both very good and very bad teams during his 15 years, but much of the time he was in the shadow of others such as Wild Bill Hallahan, Dizzy Dean, Bucky Walters, Hank Borowy and Hank Wyse. A career-for-career comparison gives the edge to Derringer in most cases, but when they were teammates the others were always just a bit better.

A couple of examples: In 1931, with the Cardinals, rookie Derringer won 18, lost 8 and had a league-leading winning percentage of .692. Hallahan went 19-9, led the league in strikeouts and won two games in leading the Cardinals to a World Series victory (Paul was 0-2). In 1939, with the Reds, Derringer was 25-7, again leading the league with a .781 percentage. But Walters topped the league with 27 wins and a 2.29 ERA and was named National League MVP.

Yet in terms of career totals, Derringer out-won them all, winning 223 times, despite playing on some wretched St Louis and Cincinnati teams in the mid 30s.

In all, he played for four pennant-winning teams. And each time he was the number two pitcher on the staff of the team in question.

Murry Dickson

Murry Monroe Dickson

If a poll had been taken of the major league pitchers of the late 1940s and 1950s as to whether they would prefer serving in Korea or performing for the Pirates, the answers, even among conscientious objectors, might have been evenly divided. Murry Dickson both served in World War II and played for the Pirates, and both ordeals probably prevented him from amassing 200 wins and maybe being elected to the Hall of Fame.

He originally came up with the powerful Cardinals of the early 1940s, but he then lost two years to the war. By 1946, when he rejoined the Cards, he was 29 and had only 14 victories.

The Pirates had finished fourth in 1948, and it appeared that they might be on the verge of making a run for the pennant, so they shelled out the huge (for the time) sum of $125,000 for Dickson to help bolster a shaky pitching staff. He *became* the staff, and for three straight years he was the only Pirate to win in double figures, and the only one to win over eight games. He won 20 in 1951, with a winning percentage of .556; the Pirates were .373 without him. The next year he dropped to 14 wins and .400, but without him the team was .235. (The 1952 Pirates can make a strong argument for the ranking as baseball's worst ever.)

In 18 seasons, Murry relieved nearly as often as he started. He retired with a 172-181 record.

Don Drysdale

Donald Scott Drysdale

The righthanded half of the most imposing mound duo (with Sandy Koufax) of recent times, Don Drysdale stood an intimidating 6'5" and dared the batters to dig in against his bullet-like side-arm deliveries.

He was considered by many to have the best spitter in history, though he never admitted to it while he was active. In 1968, pitching for the LA Dodgers, he used his full repertoire to hurl an incredible six consecutive shutouts and 58 straight scoreless innings, both of them records at the time.

Probably his best season was 1962, when he won 25 games for the Dodgers and got the Cy Young Award. He had 23 wins in 1965, and from 1962 through 1965 he won 85 games.

Almost every year he was among the leader in games started and innings pitched. But the work load finally took its toll. His strong right shoulder gave out in 1969, and he retired at the age of 33.

He had pitched for the Dodgers for 14 years. During that time he had won 203 times. His ERA was a stingy 2.95. He entered the Hall of Fame in 1984.

Dennis Eckersley

Dennis Lee Eckersley

Right and below: *Relief pitcher Dennis Eckersley's control is legendary: he walked only 55 batters in the six years from 1987 to 1992. He was originally a starter, and in his rookie season (1975) with the Cleveland Indians he was the Rookie Pitcher of the Year.*

Above left: *Murry Dickson pitched for the Pirates in the late 1940s and early 1950s.*

Below left: *Don Drysdale of the Dodgers fired his way to the Hall of Fame.*

The list of pitchers who had both 20-win and 20-save seasons is a very short one: Ellis Kinder and Dennis Eckersley.

'Eck,' the American League Rookie Pitcher of the Year in 1975, has had two careers. In the first, from 1975 through 1986, he was a starting pitcher. It wasn't until 1986, after 12 seasons and more than 350 games, that he made a relief appearance. In 1987, he embarked on his second career, that of relief pitcher *par excellence*. That season he was acquired by the Oakland Athletics and manager Tony LaRusso, trying to revive the franchise, made two highly controversial moves: he converted Dave Stewart, a reliever of little success, to a starter, and made Eckersley, a starter who had fallen on hard times, into a reliever.

And it worked. Stewart went on to win 20 games four straight years, and Eck saved an AL record 323 games, plus 30 in the NL. Back in the National League in 1996, he was the bullpen stopper of the Central Division champion St. Louis Cardinals.

Eck's best year so far was 1992: 7-1, 1.91 ERA, 51 saves, MVP and Cy Young awards. Through 1996, his win total is 192; he may become the first pitcher ever to have both 200 wins and 200 saves.

Red Faber

Urban Clarence Faber

A pitcher who was doomed to spend his entire career with the White Sox, Red Faber was, from 1923 on, a teammate of Ted Lyons for 11 seasons. It's hard to imagine a team that miserable having two Hall of Fame pitchers for so long. Just to give you an idea, during the whole time Faber and Lyons were on the same staff, the White Sox made it to the first division only once.

The redhead had one advantage over Lyons: He started sooner. He joined the Sox in 1914, and from 1915 through 1920 the team had the best record in the American League. But the players they lost after the 1920 season as a result of the Black Sox scandal were the cause of their downfall.

Faber was the World Series hero for the champion 1917 team, winning three games over the Giants and establishing the record for innings pitched in a six-game Series (27). He did not appear in the infamous 1919 World Series, so he was free of the taint that blighted the careers of some of his teammates.

He won 25 games for his seventh-place club in 1921, and he had three other 20-win seasons en route to a career of 254-212. Like Lyons, he was not a strikeout pitcher, relying on the movement of his spitball to prevent the batters from getting good wood on the ball. He was, in fact, the last AL pitcher to throw the spitball legally.

Below and right: *White Sox pitcher Red Faber won three games against the Giants in the 1917 Series and had four 20-win seasons.*

Far right: *Bob 'Rapid Robert' Feller follows through on a pitch. In his first major league game Feller struck out 15 batters. He would go on to lead the league in wins six times.*

Bob Feller

Robert William Andrew Feller

Nothing from the late 1930s to the late 1940s could stop Rapid Robert. Nothing, that is, except the global conflagration known as World War II.

Bob spent 1942-43-44 and most of 1945 in the service of our country. In the three years just prior to his enlistment, he won 24, 27 and 29 games. In the two full years after his return, he won 26 and 20. In those same five seasons he struck out 1311 batters. It is not hard to imagine that in the nearly four years he lost he might have had 90 more wins and 1000 more Ks.

Bob joined the Indians in 1936 at age 17, fresh out of high school. At 19 he was an established starter and led the American League in strikeouts for the first of seven times. His top K-season was 348 in 1946. At one time he held the record for strikeouts in a game (18) and in two consecutive games (28).

He also holds the major league record for one-hitters (12, one of which he lost). And he threw three no-hitters, including the only opening day no-hitter in history.

His career: 266 wins, 2581 Ks, four years lost.

Trivia: Who was the only regular player in the AL in 1946 whom Feller did not whiff?

Answer: Barney McCosky of the Tigers and As.

Wes Ferrell

Wesley Cheek Ferrell

Right: *Wes Ferrell was a batting as well as a pitching threat. Ferrell recorded 25 wins and a 3.31 ERA in 1930.*

Far right: *Best known for his World Series performances with Oakland in the early 1970s, Rollie Fingers is also fondly remembered for his handlebar moustache. With the Milwaukee Brewers in 1981, he led the AL with 28 saves and a 1.04 ERA, took the Brewers to their first postseason appearance, and won the MVP and Cy Young awards.*

A candidate for best hitter among baseball's top pitchers, Wes Ferrell holds both the single season (9) and career (38) home run records for his position. Add a .280 average and 208 RBI's in 1176 at bats, and his batting record will stand against anyone's.

So will his pitching record. In his 10 full seasons he won 190 games and lost but 123 for middle-of-the-pack teams that were never above third and never below sixth. After brief trials in 1927 and 1928, he joined the Indians in 1929 and proceeded to win from 21 to 25 games for his first four seasons. A sore arm in 1933 greatly reduced his effectiveness and delayed his 1934 debut, and when he was sound again he had been traded to the Red Sox.

He regained his old form in 1935 and won 25 and 20 the next two seasons. Of his contemporaries, only Lefty Grove had more 20-win seasons than Ferrell's total of six. In 15 years, he totaled 193 wins.

He had an overall winning percentage of .601. And this was on teams that were usually around .500.

Wes' catching brother, Rick, is in the Hall of Fame. A good many people think Wes should join him.

Rollie Fingers

Roland Glen Fingers

Once upon a time in the Land of Baseball, there dwelt a young clean-shaven starting pitcher who possessed rare treasures – a good sinking fastball and a hard slider, both of which could be hurled for strikes. He had come from the Land of the Bushes to the Kingdom of Oakland with glowing credentials to present to the Royal Court of King Charlie Finley. But, alas, the youthful Sir Rollie was of the nervous ilk and could not withstand the pressures of knowing a day in advance that he was to face the enemy. On nights before doing battle the young paladin would be unable to sleep, and as a result of this regrettable indisposition the next day he would be creamed.

But the Ballad of Rollie Fingers had a happy ending. Unable to stand the pressure of starting, he for some reason found the much more severe pressure of relieving to be just what he needed. He began having moderate success, and then, in the early 1970s, after Charlie Finley had the As grow facial hair, Fingers suddenly became the dominant reliever in the game.

The psychology of all this may be a little hard to fathom, but the fact remains that, glowering out from behind his big handlebar mustache as he stalked the mound, he now seemed more as if he were looking for the Dalton Gang rather than for a batter. Over 17 seasons the tall righthander saved a then-record 341 games and had 107 relief victories in 944 games. In 1981 he was named MVP and Cy Young winner in the American League. He entered the Hall of Fame in 1992.

Whitey 'The Chairman of the Board' Ford

Edward Charles Ford

You name the World Series pitching statistic – wins, losses, games, starts, innings, hits, walks, strikeouts – and chances are Whitey Ford is the all-time leader. And he's second in shutouts and fourth in complete games. Add to that the most consecutive scoreless innings in Series play. Of course, he played for the phenomenal Yankee teams of the 1950s and early 1960s – 13 pennants in 15 years – so the opportunities were certainly there, but this was a man who was at his best when the chips were down.

He joined the resident New York firm of Allie Reynolds, Vic Raschi and Ed Lopat early in the 1950 season and proceeded to compile a 9-1 record with a 2.81 ERA. Uncle Sam fed him during 1951 and 1952, and on his return in 1953 it was as if he had never left. From then through 1965 he won over 70 percent of his contests. Especially outstanding were his seasons of 1961, with 25 wins and the Cy Young Award, and 1963, when his record was 24-7.

A shoulder injury had plagued him in 1957, and it flared up again in 1966, effectively ending his reign as 'Chairman of the Board.' The classy southpaw retired during the 1967 season with a lifetime record of 236-106 and an ERA of 2.75, the best of any pitcher in the live-ball era.

Above: *Whitey Ford, brought up from the Kansas City farm team in 1950, rose quickly to the top of the Yankees' staff.*

Left: *The legendary Ford captured a Cy Young Award in 1961, with 25 wins.*

Above right: *St Louis Cardinals' pitcher Bob Gibson helped his team win two World Series during his career and won two Cy Young Awards.*

Below right: *Gibson struck out 17 batters in the first game of the 1968 World Series and tallied 3117 total whiffs by retirement.*

Bob 'Hoot' Gibson

Robert Gibson

One of the finest all-around athletes the game has known, Bob Gibson was a superb basketball player as well. His National League rivals of the 1960s and early 1970s wish he had chosen that sport.

After spending parts of two seasons with the Cardinals, he joined them for keeps in 1961, and by the next year he had established himself as one of the top pitchers in the league. *Competitor* is the word that best described him.

But tough as he was during the regular season (20 wins five times, 19 twice), possibly no one was ever better in post-season play. He led the Redbirds to World Championships in both 1964 and 1967, and only the brilliant performance of the Tigers' Mickey Lolich stopped him from doing it again in 1968.

The 1967 World Series was his greatest. His three complete game victories and his ERA of 1.00 sent the Red Sox home losers. And in 1968 he set both the single game and total Series strikeout records, 17 and 35, respectively. In Series play he hurled seven straight wins, eight straight complete games, struck out 92, walked but 17 in 81 innings and threw two shutouts.

But he was much more than a post-season phenomenon. For his career he won 251 games, 22 of them in 1968, when he had 268 strikeouts, an ERA of 1.12 and 13 shutouts. He won two Cy Young Awards.

Lefty 'Goofy,' 'The Gay Castilian' Gomez

Vernon Louis Gomez

Probably as well known for his antics and sense of humor as he was for his pitching prowess, Lefty Gomez was the Yankees' ace for the whole decade of the 1930s.

He joined the Yankees for good in 1931 and won 21 games, the first of four 20-win seasons. His best season was truly great: In 1934 he led in wins (26), percentage (.839), complete games (25), innings (282), strikeouts (158), shutouts (6) and ERA (2.33). He was the leader in shutouts and strikeouts on two other occasions, and he led in ERA again in 1937, once again with 2.33.

A sore arm in 1940, when he was only 30, marked the beginning of the end, and he left the Yankees two years later with 189 lifetime wins and a record six wins against no losses in World Series competition.

Once, when Bob Feller was at his fastest and his wildest, Gomez stepped into the batter's box against him late in a game. He dug into his pocket, pulled out a match and lit it. 'What's wrong?' asked the umpire, 'Can't you see?' 'I can see just fine,' replied Lefty. 'I just want to be sure *he* can see me.'

Opposite: *Lefty Gomez, ace pitcher for the Yankees in the 1930s.*

Above: *Gomez shows the intensity that enabled him to produce four 20-win seasons and dominate just about every pitching category in 1934.*

Goose Gossage

Richard Michael Gossage

The young flamethrowing righthander Rich Gossage spent several major league seasons trying to find himself (ERA in the vicinity of 5.00). Then one day it all came together. In 1975 he let the world know he was there by making 62 appearances with 26 saves and establishing a 1.84 ERA. But it took more than that to save the poor old White Sox in those days.

The new manager, Paul Richards, converted him to a starter in 1976. Richards had a reputation as a fine molder and handler of pitchers, but this was one of his lesser brainstorms. The move deprived the Chisox of their bullpen stopper, and it did nothing to improve the rotation. That year they finished last, and their failed starter was traded.

Rich rejoined his former manager, Chuck Tanner, with the NL in Pittsburgh, and Tanner, who made him a reliever in the first place, returned him to the bullpen. That year, 1977, his ERA was 1.62. The following year he put on the uniform of the New York Yankees and would go on wearing it for the next six seasons. His ERA in his first year with the Bombers was 2.01, and he was credited with one of the four Series wins that made the team the 1978 World Champions.

Rich became Goose along the way and he pitched through the 1994 season. At the end, he was one of only a handful of men to top 300 saves (310), 100 relief wins (115 of his 124 came out of the bullpen) and 1000 games on the mound (1002). He was the AL Fireman of the Year in both 1975 and 1978, and in 1977 he set the single-season record for strikeouts in relief (151).

Above: *Burly righthander Goose Gossage of the Yankees won Game 4 of the 1978 Series.*

Opposite: *Gossage, as a relief pitcher in 1977 with Pittsburgh, had a 1.62 ERA.*

Burleigh 'Ol' Stubblebeard' Grimes

Burleigh Arland Grimes

Burleigh Grimes was a good-hitting pitcher – one of the best, for he had over 30 hits in four different seasons. As a hitter he also set a record that may never be broken: On 22 September 1925 he hit into two double plays and a triple play.

Said to be the very last major league pitcher to legally throw the spitball, he went on for 14 more years after his bread-and-butter pitch was banned. He used the wet one to win 20 games five times. He got 25 with the 1928 Pirates, and he hit 19 twice. For most of the 1920s he was the ace of an essentially second division Dodgers team, but he became somewhat nomadic later, making eight uniform changes in his final eight seasons.

He was one of a handful of pitchers to win 13 consecutive games – for the Giants in 1927. Yet he was also one of a smaller number to lose that many in a row; this he did for the 1917 Pirates.

But that was only his rookie season, when his record was 3 and 16. After a 19-year career, Ol' Stubblebeard had won 270 games, and in 1931 he led the Cardinals to a World Championship.

Lefty 'Mose' Grove

Robert Moses Grove

In the early 1920s Lefty Grove pitched for the then-minor league Baltimore Orioles, and he posted some of the most impressive statistics the International League had ever seen. This was perhaps the greatest of all minor league teams, and it was so successful financially that it felt no great urgency to part with any of its top stars. So it was not until Lefty was 25 that Connie Mack was able to persuade the Orioles to sell him to the Athletics for the record sum of $100,600.

It took him two more years to conquer his control problems. After that . . . the word *dominance* comes to mind. For seven consecutive seasons, 1927-1933, he won 20 or more games, topped by a 31-4 record in 1931. He was, in fact, the last American Leaguer to win 30 until Denny McLain did it in 1968. During his first seven years he also led the league in strikeouts, equalling Dazzy Vance's record. After he was traded to the Red Sox in 1934 he added another 20-win season in the very next year.

Grove spent 17 years in the American League. In nine of those years he led the league in ERA and five years in winning percentage. He closed out his career in 1941 with exactly 300 wins. It requires no soul searching to rank this great Hall of Fame pitcher in the Top Ten.

Opposite: *Spitballer Burleigh Grimes was hardly ever this clean-shaven.*

Right: *Lefty Grove dominated the AL during his tenure with the As and Red Sox.*

35

Ron 'Gator', 'Louisiana Lightning' Guidry

Ronald Ames Guidry

Primarily a relief pitcher in the minors, and not a very effective one, Ron Guidry spent most of six years in the Yankee chain. Trials with the parent club in 1975 and 1976 were uninspired, but when he was sent down to Syracuse in early 1976 he was nearly unhittable, allowing only 16 hits in 40 innings over 22 games.

Finally, in 1977, at the age of 27, he went to the Yankees to stay, but despite his relief credentials at Syracuse, manager Billy Martin put the thin lefthander in the starting rotation. Before the season was over Ron was the staff ace, leading the team in wins (16), strikeouts (176) and ERA (2.82).

In 1978 he produced one of the finest seasons in modern memory: 25-3, with a .893 percentage (the highest ever for a 20-game winner), a 1.74 ERA, nine shutouts and 248 strikeouts. For that he got the Cy Young Award.

The relationship between 'Louisiana Lightning' and the Yankees' front office was not always the rosiest. After the 1981 season he chose free agency, but rejoined the Yankees in December. After 1986 he again went the free agency route. Whether or not because of collusion (as he charged), he went unsigned. He rejoined New York in May 1987.

He retired during the 1988 season with 170 wins against 91 losses, an outstanding .651 percentage, fourth best of the live-ball era among pitchers with at least 150 career wins.

Mel 'Chief,' 'Wimpy' Harder

Melvin LeRoy Harder

The Indians of the 1930s and early 1940s were not a bad team. Nor were they a good team. In the 16 years from 1930 through 1945, they were fourth or fifth ten times and third five times. Mel Harder spent his entire career with this team.

The owner of a great breaking ball, he was not a strikeout pitcher and his control, while good, was not great. He consistently gave up more hits than innings pitched. In 20 seasons, the only thing he ever led in was shutouts (six in 1934). But he won on 223 occasions, 20 twice, and that's what it's all about.

Many claim the 1954 Indians had the best pitching staff in history: Bob Lemon, Early Wynn, Mike Garcia, Art Houtteman, Bob Feller, Hal Newhouser, Don Mossi and Ray Narleski. Houtteman and Newhouser had appeared to be washed up in Detroit. Mossi and Narleski were rookies who had been minor league starters, and the zip in Feller's arm was gone, and his starts had to be carefully chosen. Yet those five gave the Tribe a record of 44-16, with 27 saves. Their pitching coach was Mel Harder.

Trivia: What pitcher has the best All-Star game record?

Answer: You guessed it – 13 innings, no runs.

Opposite: *1978 was a banner year for lefthander Ron Guidry of the New York Yankees. He won the Cy Young Award that year, posting 25 wins, a 1.74 ERA and a .893 winning percentage.*

Right: *Cleveland pitcher Mel Harder won 223 games for the Indians from 1928-1947 and coached the Indians' famous pitching staff in 1954.*

Waite 'Schoolboy' Hoyt

Waite Charles Hoyt

Another of the many Red Sox contributions to the Yankees' success in the 1920s, Waite Hoyt had an integral part in the forming of one of baseball's great dynasties. Joining the Bombers in 1921, he helped them to six pennants and three World Championships in the next eight years. He was called 'Schoolboy' because at 15 he was pitching batting practice for the Dodgers and Giants, and John McGraw signed him for a $5 bonus in 1916, when Waite was 16. Hoyt's father was upset; he felt $5 was too much money for a boy of that age to carry around.

He was still only 21 when he joined the Yankees, but he won 19 games for them the first year and eventually topped the 20 mark twice. He was not a strikeout artist, only twice in 21 seasons surpassing 100, but good control and belief in his fielders' abilities led him to 237 wins in his career. As a Yankee he had a .616 winning percentage.

He added six World Series victories and ranks high in most Series statistics. He was inducted into the Hall of Fame in 1969.

Left: *Wait Hoyt.* **Right:** *Carl Hubbell of the Giants pitched five consecutive 21-or-more-wins seasons.*

Below: *Hoyt posted 237 career wins.*

Carl 'King Carl,' 'The Meal Ticket' Hubbell

Carl Owen Hubbell

The 1934 All-Star game saw the birth of one of baseball's great legends: King Carl Hubbell struck out five of the greatest hitters in the history of the game in succession. Mowed down by the great screwballer were Babe Ruth, Lou Gehrig, Jimmie Foxx, Al Simmons, and Joe Cronin.

Hubbell was originally a property of the Tigers, but manager Ty Cobb didn't see much in the young lefty in the early 1920s. John McGraw of the Giants took a look a few years later and had a different opinion.

Hubbell, at the age of 25, joined the Giants in 1928 in mid-season and went on to win 10 games. Before long, and for obvious reasons, his teammates began calling him 'The Meal Ticket.' He led the Giants to a World

Championship in 1933 and to National League pennants in 1936 and 1937.

As long as his arm was sound, the Giants were always in contention. During his first 10 years, with the sole exception of 1932 (the year McGraw passed the reins to Bill Terry), Hubbell and the Giants were never below third place. But in 1938 Hubbell developed a sore arm, and it curbed his effectiveness for the remainder of his career. For those six years the Giants, not coincidentally, became a second division club. He ended his 16-year career with 253 wins.

To further illustrate his impact, he was the first pitcher to be named MVP on two occasions, 1933 and 1936. He has been in the Hall of Fame since 1947.

Catfish Hunter

James Augustus Hunter

When Charles Finley signed Jim Hunter to his first contract, he asked the young righthander if he had a nickname. Finley liked nicknames. He had just signed 'Blue Moon' Odom, and when he learned that Hunter was called only Jim, Finley dubbed him 'Catfish'. (A few years later, after Finley signed Vida Blue, he offered him a bonus if he would change his name to 'True'.)

Hunter spent his only year in the minors on the disabled list. He joined the As' rotation at the age of 19 in 1965 in Kansas City and developed along with the other young players. When these youngsters matured a few years later, they turned the Oakland As into baseball's last true dynasty which won five consecutive American League West titles between 1971 and 1975, as well as three straight World Series between 1972 and 1974.

The ace of the staff was Jim Hunter. He topped off four straight 20-win seasons for the As with a league-leading 25 and a Cy Young Award in 1974. Declared a free agent at the end of that season due to a contract clause not being fulfilled, he signed with the Yankees and led the league again with 23 victories, his fifth 20-win season. When he retired at the age of only 33, following the 1979 season, he had a lifetime total of 224 wins in the regular season and nine more in post-season play. He was elected to the Hall of Fame in 1987.

Ferguson Jenkins

Ferguson Arthur Jenkins

When one thinks of Ferguson Jenkins, one associates him with the Cubs, right? Six consecutive 20-win seasons, Cy Young winner in 1971, annually among the strikeout leaders. But who holds most of the Texas Rangers' pitching records? The temptation is to say Charlie Hough, but the name at the top of this page probably precludes one from saying that too loudly.

One of the premier control pitchers of modern times, Fergie walked fewer than two batters per nine innings for his 19-year career. His strikeouts to walks ratio was a superb 3.2:1 and he is one of a handful of pitchers to whiff over 3000 men, and he is the *only* one with over 3000 strikeouts and fewer than 1000 bases on balls.

He put together one of the over-all best seasons since World War II in his Cy Young year of 1971: 24 wins, 30 complete games, 325 innings, 37 walks (one per nine innings), 263 Ks (a 7.1:1 ratio) and six home runs as a batter.

Equally good was 1974, his first year with the Rangers. He had a total of 25 wins, 29 complete games, 328 innings, 45 walks (1.2 per nine) and 245 Ks for a 5.4:1 ratio.

He rounded out his career back in Chicago with some pretty bad Cubs teams in 1982 and 1983, finishing with 284 wins. He was honored with Hall of Fame induction in 1991.

Above: *Jim 'Catfish' Hunter won 25 games and a Cy Young Award in 1974.*

Overleaf (p42): *Hunter pitching his perfect game for the As in 1968.*

Opposite: *Ferguson Jenkins, shown here winding up for the Chicago Cubs in 1982, ranks with the best of the control pitchers.*

Tommy John

Thomas Edward John

Up and down for two years, Tommy John came to the majors to stay in 1965, joining the White Sox from the Indians in a three-club deal that also involved the Athletics. From then until 1974 the southpaw was a dependable, if not spectacular, starter for the Pale Hose and the Dodgers.

But in 1974 he appeared to be on his way to a banner season, with a 13-3 record by mid-July. But then one pitch almost ended it all. 'I felt like my hand, wrist and forearm had left my elbow,' Tommy said later. A ligament had ruptured, and with it a nerve had been damaged. The general opinion was that he would never pitch again. He missed the remainder of 1974 and all of 1975, but miraculous transplant surgery proved successful, and Tommy pitched 14 more years, until he was 46.

In the 12 years before the injury, John won 124 games, but he never won more than 16 in a season. In 14 years after surgery, he won 164 times with three 20-win seasons. His 26 years as a major league pitcher is second only to Nolan Ryan's 27; his lost 1975 season would have enabled him to share the record and undoubtedly make it to the 300-win level.

Opposite: *Tommy John as a Yankee in 1979.*

Above: *Lefthander Tommy John of the Dodgers, 1975.*

Walter 'The Big Train,' 'Barney' Johnson

Walter Perry Johnson

'The most fearsome sight I had ever seen in a baseball uniform.' That's how Ty Cobb described Walter Johnson when Cobb reminisced about facing the rookie pitcher in his major league debut in 1907. The Tigers beat the 19-year-old Johnson that day because of the young pitcher's inexperience in fielding bunts, but that failed to cool the enthusiasm of Cobb. He tried to convince Tiger management to acquire Johnson in any manner they could. Had he been able to convince them, perhaps it would have enabled Cobb to play for the Series winner that eluded him throughout his career.

The Big Train pitched 21 years for the Washington Senators. In 11 of those seasons the team finished below .500, and for Johnson's career they lost more than they won. But with a sub-.500 team, Johnson had a .599 winning percentage. His 416 career victories are the second most in history, and his 5923 innings are the most anyone has pitched exclusively in the twentieth century. He is the only pitcher in history to throw over 100 shutouts. He pitched and won an amazing 38 1-0 games.

Sophisticated timing devices were not available in his day, but those who saw him say he was the fastest pitcher of them all. His 3508 career strikeouts stood as the record for over half a century. And that wasn't all. He could hit: All told, he belted in 24 home runs, for a .236 career average.

Sad Sam Jones

Samuel Pond Jones

Sad Sam Jones is not to be confused with the fine National League hurler of the 1950s of the same name and nickname. This Sam was another of the many pitchers who made the infamous Boston to New York run in the late teens and early 1920s. Sad Sam Jones lent his strong right arm to the Yankee cause for five years. During that period they won three pennants.

Perhaps Jones' best season came in 1921. That year the Red Sox finished an uninspired fifth in the American League with a record of 75-79, but Sam was 23-16 and led the American League in shutouts with five. He was a 20-game winner one other time, leading the 1923 Yanks into the Series with a 21-5 record. Unfortunately, his record for the Series itself was 0-1.

In 22 seasons, Sam hurled for six of the then-extant eight AL clubs – New York, Cleveland, Boston, St Louis, Washington and Chicago - missing only the Athletics and the Tigers. A pretty good hitter, his average dropped below .200 only at the end of his career.

In all, he racked up 229 major league wins, including a no-hitter in 1923. Which, when you come to think of it, is nothing to be sad about.

Opposite: *Walter Johnson pitched for the Senators 21 years, with 416 wins.*

Right: *Sam Jones took the Yanks to the World Series in 1923 with a 21-5 record.*

Addie Joss

Adrian Joss

Would Addie Joss have been considered one of the all-time greats if he had played longer? Such speculations are usually pointless, but in Joss' case the evidence is more than usually intriguing.

His career was limited to fewer than nine full seasons, but he won 20 or more games four times. And he won those consecutively. He also totalled 160 victories in that short span, including one no-hitter and one perfect game.

The most remarkable aspect of Addie's career was his ERA. The *highest* it ever was was in his rookie year, 1902, when he had a 17-13 record for a Cleveland team that was under .500 without him. His ERA that season was 2.77. The next highest was in his last (partial) season in 1910. That year, when he was a dying man, he finished at 2.26. In between, he had five seasons of 1.83 and under, and his career ERA of 1.88 is the second best in the history of the game.

Joss died early in 1911, at the age of 31, from tubercular meningitis. To illustrate the regard in which he was held by his peers, the first All-Star game was held in an attempt to raise some money for his family.

Addie Joss was elected to the Hall of Fame in 1978.

Right: *Addie Joss, a Cleveland Indians pitcher from 1902 to 1910, pitched a perfect game against the Chicago White Sox in 1908, and that year led the AL with a 1.16 ERA.*

Opposite: *Lefthander Jim Kaat, a 25-year veteran of the major leagues, won 16 consecutive Gold Glove awards.*

Jim Kaat

James Lee Kaat

Jim Kaat was the first pitcher in major league history to ply his trade for 25 years.

A model of consistency, from 1962 through 1976 he won 227 games, despite stints on the disabled list with arm trouble and a broken wrist. The bulk of that time he was the Twins' stopper, and he still holds many Minnesota pitching records. A three-time 20-game winner, he topped the league with 25 in 1966.

Kaat was more than a great pitcher. He ranks with such as Bob Lemon and Bob Gibson as among the best at all aspects of the game. Though he had only a .185 batting average, Jim was nevertheless highly respected as a batter – understandably, since he banged out 16 homers over his career.

To round out his status as the complete pitcher, the redheaded southpaw was awarded 16 consecutive Gold Gloves for fielding excellence, a record unlikely to be approached by any other pitcher. He had no peer at going to his right off the mound.

After 25 seasons, he had appeared in 898 games, placing him fifth in history in this category. And he won 283 of them.

Sandy Koufax

Sanford Koufax

Signed by the Brooklyn Dodgers as a bonus baby from the University of Cincinnati in December 1954, Sandy was required by the prevailing rules to remain with the team for two years. He was only 18, and he was a long way in performance and years from what he was to become. During his two years of forced servitude he won four and lost six, and in 1957 it was decided to send him down for needed experience. The assignment was announced but never fulfilled. Sandy never spent a day in the minors.

1958 saw the Dodgers move to Los Angeles. Experience had helped, and Koufax joined the rotation, but very few sober people could see the Hall of Fame in the young southpaw's future. After six full seasons, he had an uninspiring record of 36-40 and an ERA over 4.00.

But in 1961 he began to achieve a dominance the likes of which had rarely been approached in the past and has not been seen since. Over a six year period he won 129, lost only 47 (.733), struck out 1713 in 1632 innings, hurled four no-hitters (including a perfect game), won three Cy Young Awards, led in ERA five consecutive years and set the single season strikeout record (since broken by Nolan Ryan).

At the end of this reign he was only 30 years old. But his arthritis was by then so severe that he chose to retire rather than face the pain any longer.

In his final season (1966) he was 27-9 with 317 Ks and an ERA of 1.73. There's only one thing you can say about a performance like that: What a way to go.

Above: *Sandy Koufax pitched in four Series with the LA Dodgers. He posted 11 shutouts in 1963.*

Opposite: *Ray Kremer led the Pirates to two pennants and a World Championship in 1925.*

Ray 'Wiz' Kremer

Remy Peter Kremer

Born and raised in Oakland, California, Ray Kremer as a boy dreamed of pitching for the Oaks. At 21 he signed a contract with Sacramento, not far away. Over the next three years he worked for several minor league teams, including San Francisco, but in 1916 he found himself on the other end of the world in Rochester, NY. He requested either his release or sale to a team on the Pacific coast. He was obliged.

1917 found him home in Oakland. He stayed there seven years, winning over 100 games for the Oaks and refusing several opportunities to move to a higher level. In 1924, however, Pittsburgh offered both Oakland and Kremer money that could not be refused.

Ray had subtracted three years from his age when he originally signed, feeling 21 was too old to be starting a career, so the Pirates thought they were getting a 28-year-old rookie in 1924. Instead they got a 31-year-old who carried their staff for nearly a decade.

Kremer led the National League in victories twice with 20, in both 1926 and 1930. From 1924 through 1930 he won 127, lost only 67 and led the Bucs to two pennants and one Series Championship (in 1925, over the Washington Senators).

In less than 10 years as a Pirate, Ray went 143-85 for a .627 winning percentage. It's a pity he didn't get into the majors sooner.

Bob Lemon

Robert Granville Lemon

When Bob Lemon went off to serve in World War II he left baseball as a third baseman-outfielder. When he returned in 1946 he was a pitcher. He established himself on the Cleveland Indians' staff in 1947, at age 26, joined the rotation the next season and produced the best record of any pitcher in baseball over the next decade.

Over a nine-year period he won 20 or more games seven times, and on one occasion when he missed 20 he still led the American League with 18 victories. These were excellent Indian teams, annually at or near the top of the standings. They had some top pitchers – Feller, Wynn, Garcia, Bearden, Score – but the one constant on the staff was Lemon. For the nine years, 1948-1956, he went 186-106 and led the AL in wins three times, in complete games five times and in innings four times. In 1948 he tossed ten shutouts.

Aiding his strong right arm was his formidable bat. One of the top hitting pitchers in history, he had a career batting average of .232, with 37 homers. A frequent pinch-hitter, his average in these situations was an outstanding .284.

Bob pitched for 13 years and retired with 207 wins. His percentage was .618, and his ERA 3.23. He became a Hall of Famer in 1976.

Right: *Bob Lemon pitched for the Cleveland Indians from 1946 to 1958. He was a formidable hitter as well as a leading AL pitcher, retiring with 207 wins. He later managed in the majors.*

Opposite: *'Dutch' Leonard kept batters guessing with a mixture of curveballs, knuckleballs and fastballs.*

Emil 'Dutch' Leonard

Emil John Leonard

Two Dutch Leonards pitched major league baseball, and very well, at that. Dutch I set the all-time single season standard with a 1.01 ERA for the 1914 Red Sox. This, however, concerns Dutch II. His 20-year career spanned the years 1933-1953. In that time he played on only two teams that finished above .500, yet he won 20 games in 1939 and 14 to 18 in six more seasons.

Dutch was probably the premier knuckleballer of his day, but he also had a good curve and fastball. How good his command of all of them was is suggested by the fact that he averaged only two walks per nine innings. He was among the top starters for a dozen years, but he finished up in the Cubs' bullpen as one of the National League's top relievers.

In spite of the usually inept supporting casts behind him, Dutch held his own, and only a broken ankle suffered in 1942, limiting him to six games, stopped him from winning 200 games. Leonard won 190, with a winning percentage of .513, for teams that only averaged a mediocre .449.

Mickey Lolich

Michael Stephen Lolich

Mickey Lolich is listed in one prominent baseball reference book as 6'1" and 170 pounds. That may have been his birth weight, but any Tigers fan of the late 1960s through the mid-1970s will tell you that Mickey's girth was almost as large as his talent.

Whatever his real weight, at the peak of his career Lolich gave hope to all potbellied armchair athletes as he blew by American League batters with his blazing fastball. Twice he won 20 games, topped by 25 in 1971, and he struck out more batters than any southpaw in AL history – 2679. Seven times (six in a row) he whiffed over 200, leading the world in 1971 with 308. Also in 1971, he hurled 376 innings, the most by any

one to that time in the live ball era.

He was considered just another good pitcher in 1964, his first full season, but in the 1968 World Series he showed his greatness. He led the Tigers to victory over the heavily favored Cardinals by hurling three complete game victories, including out-dueling the brilliant Bob Gibson in the seventh game. Other highlights: In the second game he hit the only home run of his career, and in the seventh he picked both Lou Brock and Curt Flood off first base in the same inning.

Mickey rounded (in more ways than one) out his career in the National League with 217 wins (207 as a Tiger). In all, he had 2832 strikeouts.

Ed 'Steady Eddie' Lopat

Edmund Walter Lopat

Casey Stengel once said of Eddie Lopat, 'I hate it when he pitches; guys come out of the stands wanting contracts 'cause they can throw harder than he can.' Lopat had a fastball, but he also had a curve that he could throw at several speeds, a screwball and a slider, all of which he threw with the same easy, effortless motion that earned him the unofficial nickname of 'Junkman.'

Lopat came to the majors with the horrible White Sox of the mid-1940s. (Things were so bad that the year after Lopat left, Frank Lane put the whole team on waivers, just to see if anyone would want them. Only one player was claimed.) In 1948 new Yankee general manager George Weiss, in his first trade, sent three men to Chicago in exchange for Ed.

Relying on control and intelligence, as well as his variety of pitches, the stocky lefthander fashioned a record of 113-59 (.657) in seven and a half years in New York, including a 21-9 log in 1951. And perhaps as important as his pitching was his steadying influence on the younger pitchers, to say nothing of all that he taught them.

In 12 full seasons, Eddie won 166 games. Added to that was a 4-1 World Series record in five consecutive Series between 1949 and 1953.

Opposite: *Detroit Tiger rifler Mickey Lolich turned in a stellar performance in the 1968 World Series, winning three games (one against Bob Gibson) and even launching a home run.*

Right: *Ed Lopat appeared in five World Series with the New York Yankees, winning four games. A large variety of pitches, together with smarts and consistent control, allowed Lopat to win 166 games.*

Ted Lyons

Theodore Amar Lyons

When the bad teams of history are discussed, generally prominent in the conversations are the early Mets, the Pirates of the early 1950s, the fairly recent Cubs, the Browns and the Senators. Perhaps less likely to be included are the White Sox, but we have to bear in mind that the southside Chicago franchise, through the decades of the 1920s, 1930s and 1940s was among the most inept of all time. In the 30 years from 1921 through 1950 the Pale Hose climbed to the dizzying heights of third place on only three occasions, and in three other seasons they finished at the giddy level of fourth. Twenty-four times they were a second division club, 10 times either seventh or eighth.

Ted Lyons had the misfortune to pitch for and/or manage this team for 23 of those 30 seasons. In 21 active seasons he had a 260-230 record, a winning percentage of .531. The Sox had a percentage of .460.

Blessed with good control, he usually let the batters hit the ball; the most strikeouts he ever had in a season was 72. But he was a three-time 20-game winner and he helped his own cause by being one of the better hitting pitchers of his era, frequently being used as a pinch-hitter.

Ted pitched complete games in the final 26 appearances of his career, including all 20 times out in 1942.

Left: *Ted Lyons of the Chicago White Sox.*

Right: *Multiple Cy Young Award winner Greg Maddux.*

Greg Maddux

Gregory Alan Maddux

He may not look like a ballplayer, much less an outstanding one, but Greg Maddux may someday appear on the list of the Top Ten pitchers of all time.

Rushed to the majors at the age of 20 by the pitching-hungry Cubs, he wasn't ready and it showed. In parts of two seasons, he went 8-18 with a 5.59 ERA. But he found himself in 1988 and from then through 1996 went 157-92 with a 2.64 ERA, the best in baseball for that period. He has reached a dominance enjoyed by only a handful of pitchers at any time.

And each year he seems to be better. Through 1995, he won four consecutive Cy Young awards and by 1996 six straight Gold Gloves. He has won 20 games on two occasions, and led the National League in wins twice, in ERA twice, in innings four times (consecutively), and in complete games twice. At the end of the 1996 season, Maddux was once again one of the most outstanding pitchers in baseball. His control, always outstanding, has now reached near-perfection.

And if his arm isn't enough, his batting average is often higher than the average he allows the hitters he faces.

Juan Marichal

Juan Antonio Sanchez Marichal

This hot-tempered Dominican had the misfortune to be a contemporary of, first, Sandy Koufax and, later, Bob Gibson. On at least three occasions while with San Francisco he put up numbers that in most years would have earned the Cy Young Award, only to lose out in the balloting to those other two Hall of Famers.

From 1963 through 1969 he won 21 or more games each year except 1967, when a leg injury cost him a third of the season. (He still won 14.) His top performances came in 1963 (25-8 and an ERA of 2.41), 1966 (25-6 and an ERA of 2.23) and 1968 (26-9 and an ERA of 2.43), as he became only the second pitcher (Koufax was the other) since Hal Newhouser to have three 25-win seasons.

With a career record of 243-142 and an ERA of 2.89 over 16 seasons, Hall of Fame induction would have seemed to be a matter of course, but he had to wait until his fourth year of eligibility to be recognized. Some attribute the wait to the infamous incident in which he tried to brain Dodger catcher John Roseboro with his bat, while others blame his terrible temper and his feisty attitude towards the media.

Rube Marquard

Richard William Marquard

The Giants shocked the baseball world in January 1908 when they purchased an 18-year-old southpaw named Rube Marquard from Canton, of the Central League, for the then-extraordinary sum of $11,000. The return on that investment was slow to come, and by 1911 Marquard, still only 21, had a three-year record of 9-18. By that time many were laughing at the Giants and their expensive lemon.

But then the Giants began laughing. From 1911 through 1913, Rube won 73 games and led the Giants to three straight National League pennants. In 1912 he established the modern record for consecutive victories in a season when he reeled off 19 in a row.

Later traded to the Dodgers, he helped them to two pennants but he never had the good fortune to pitch for a Series winner. In 14 full seasons and parts of four more Rube won 201 games, but apart from his three brilliant years he was a sub-.500 pitcher. He is enshrined in the Hall of Fame, and no doubt deserves it, but you can't help wondering why several others are not there also.

Left above: *Juan Marichal had six 20-win seasons and led the NL in wins twice.*

Left below: *Dennis Martinez, now with the Indians, pitched a perfect game for Montreal in 1991.*

Right: *Rube Marquard began pitching for the New York Giants at age 18 in 1908 and pitched there until 1915. The Hall of Famer led the National League in strikeouts (237) and winning percentage (.774) in 1911, and set a record for consecutive wins in 1912 with 19.*

Dennis Martinez

José Dennis Martinez

As of 1996, Dennis Martinez had put in 21 major league seasons, but in 1986 it seemed that he was through when his shoulder gave out. He had had a nice career to that point, though. He was 32 years old and had won 108 games, all for the Baltimore Orioles.

But baseball has always been a 'what-have-you-done-for-me-lately' sport and the Orioles found a taker for Martinez and his ailing shoulder. He was traded to Montreal in mid-season of 1986 and did not do very well the rest of that season, but he 1987 he returned to his old form and through 1993 won an even 100 games for the Expos.

Back in the American League with Cleveland in 1994, his 11 wins led the rejuvenated Indians in the strike-shortened season, and in the 1995 season he was again the staff leader at the age of 40 as the Tribe won its first American League title in more than four decades.

Martinez belongs to two very exclusive clubs: the 200-win with no 20-win-season club and the 100 wins in each league club. And he pitched a perfect game in 1991. His goal now is to pitch until his son Dennis, Jr, drafted by Cleveland in 1995, makes it to the big leagues.

Christy 'Big Six' Mathewson

Christopher Mathewson

The 1905 World Series: The Giants' handsome and gentlemanly Christy Mathewson started three games against the Philadelphia Athletics. He won all three, and all three were shutouts. In 27 innings he gave up only 14 hits. He walked but one batter and struck out 18. This is far and away the greatest pitching performance the Fall Spectacular has ever seen.

All in all, 1905 had been a great year for the pitcher whom both the Athletics' Connie Mack and the Giants' John McGraw described as the best they had ever seen. He had won 30 or more games for the third year in a row, and he had led the league in strikeouts for the third consecutive season.

In 1908 he set a modern National League record for wins, with 37. He won 20 or more 13 times, 12 of those times in succession. His 373 career victories are third highest, and his percentage is a phenomenal .665.

This was an amazing pitcher, but the most amazing aspect of his performance was his control. He walked fewer than 1.6 batters per nine innings for his 17-year career. Not once in his final five seasons did he average more than one walk per nine innings.

His life was shortened by the effects of having breathed poison gas in France in World War I, and he died in 1925 at the age of 45. Baseball had lost one of its greatest players and finest men.

Left: *Christy Mathewson's nickname 'Big Six' came from New York's most famous fire engine. Mathewson brought the New York Giants five pennants; his performance in the 1905 World Series is legendary.*

Right: *Mathewson was known for his great control. In 1908 he posted 259 strikeouts in 391 innings, with only 42 walks; and in 1913 he went 68 straight innings without a walk.*

Carl 'Sub' Mays

Carl William Mays

Another in the long line of Red Sox gifts to the Yankees, Mays was already an established front-line pitcher in 1919 when Boston shipped him to New York in mid-season in exchange for $40,000 and two pitchers who, in seven seasons, had career totals of 27-38. Up to this point, the Red Sox had been a force to be reckoned with in the American League. In the league's first 18 seasons the Red Sox had won five World Championships and six pennants, and in those 18 seasons the Sox had finished in the first division 15 times. But this trade marked the beginning of the end. The Sox would not return to the first division until 1934.

Carl Mays was a hard-nosed competitor who asked no quarter and gave none. It was well-known that he would brush back a batter he thought was digging in too strongly, and on 16 August 1920 a pitch got away from him and struck Cleveland shortstop Ray Chapman in the head. He died the next day, regaining consciousness only momentarily.

This incident may be what is keeping Mays out of the Hall of Fame, for his career stats are impressive. In 15 seasons he won 208 games and had a winning percentage of .623. He won 20 or more five times.

Right: *Spitballer Carl Mays went to New York from Boston in 1919.*

Opposite left: *Lindy McDaniel of the St Louis Cardinals.*

Opposite right: *Joe McGinnity was the epitome of durability during his long career. He pitched eight straight 20-win seasons, including two 30-win seasons.*

Lindy McDaniel

Lyndall Dale McDaniel

Hoyt Wilhelm was probably the first real relief pitcher. Of course, there had been many pitchers who had been used in relief over the years and some had outstanding success for a while. Such outstanding pitchers as Hugh Casey, Joe Page, Johnny Sain, Ellis Kinder and Mace Brown were originally starters who, for various reasons, found themselves in the bullpen. But Wilhelm was the first who didn't enter the majors as a starter. The second was probably Roy Face. And Lindy McDaniel was the third. And they each relied on only one kind of pitch to get the job done.

Lindy joined the St Louis Cardinals in 1955 as a bonus baby, having never participated in a minor league game. Like Wilhelm and Face, he made some starts, but in 21 big league seasons he appeared in 987 games. He was 22-31 as a starter, but he was 119-87 in relief. Lindy led the National League in saves three times: 1959, 1960 and 1963.

He led the league in saves three times and had 172 for his career. He is second in relief wins and second in relief innings. His top single season mark for saves, made in 1970, was 29.

Joe 'Iron Man' McGinnity

Joseph Jerome McGinnity

Although his nickname came from working in steel mills, few have ever been better deserved. The Iron Man pitched a total of 26 professional seasons, off and on, from the age of 22 until he was 54. He won over 480 games and threw over 7000 innings.

Only 10 years of his career were spent at the major league level, and he was an advanced 28 years old as a rookie in 1899. But in his first eight seasons he never won fewer than 21 games, and he *averaged* nearly 25 wins for his 10 years.

Twice he won over 30 games, and twice he hurled over 400 innings. His 434 in 1903 is the modern National League record. For his first nine years he never tossed fewer than 310 innings. He led the NL in games pitched six times, and innings five times. And on five occasions he pitched *both* ends of a doubleheader; on three of these occasions he won both games.

After leaving the Giants at the end of the 1908 season he won 20 or more games per season six more times and pitched 400-plus innings three more times in the minors. His staying power and success have been attributed to a natural underhand motion from which he threw a curve that broke up instead of down. He joined the Hall of Fame in 1946.

Right: *Denny McLain, the great Detroit Tigers' hurler, shows classical pitching form in the sixth game of the 1968 World Series.*

Below: *A McLain pitch as seen from behind home base. The young rifler was the first in the majors to win 30 games (1968) since Dizzy Dean in 1934.*

Opposite: *Al Kaline helps McLain celebrate his 30th win of the 1968 season against the Oakland Athletics on 14 September.*

Denny McLain

Dennis Dale McLain

'Pitching is the easy part.' That was what Denny McLain told Mark Fidrych when 'The Bird' was flying his highest. It could well be the story of Denny's life. There have been few better, brighter starts than the one made by the brash young McLain. But by the time most pitchers are just beginning to establish themselves, his career was over.

At the age of 21, in his first year with the Tigers, he was 16-6, with a 2.61 ERA. He followed that with 20-14 and 17-16 seasons. Then came *the* season.

In 1968 Denny owned the American League. He won 31 games, to be the first 30 game winner in the majors since 1934 and the first in the American League since 1931. He was the first pitcher in the AL to win both the Cy Young and MVP Awards in the same season. Perhaps the most amazing part of the year was that he allowed only 8.1 baserunners per nine innings.

The following year he delivered another top performance. His 24 wins again led the league, and he became the first American Leaguer to win the Cy Young Award in consecutive seasons, sharing the award with Mike Cuellar of the Orioles.

But the end was in sight. Early in 1970 Commissioner Bowie Kuhn suspended him for alleged gambling, and when McLain returned, he was overweight and out of shape. Two more suspensions, for various reasons, followed, and the Denny of the late 1960s was only a memory. By 1972, at 28, he was out of baseball.

Dave McNally

David Arthur McNally

How do you decide who is the ace of a pitching staff that annually produces two to four 20-game winners? The Orioles of the late 1960s and early 1970s had this problem, one that all teams would like to be faced with.

Between 1969 and 1974, Mike Cuellar won from 18 to 24 games a year, Jim Palmer won between 16 and 22 during the years from 1969 to 1973, Pat Dobson had back-to-back seasons of 20 and 16 in 1971 and 1972 and Dave McNally put together four straight 20-win seasons from 1968 through 1971. It is no secret that this was the best pitching staff in the post-World War II era. Maybe it was the best of all time.

At several points McNally was so hot that it appeared he might never lose again. He is the only pitcher in history to have three winning streaks of 12 games or more – 12 in 1968, 15 in 1969 and 13 in 1971. He also won his last two decisions of 1968, which, when added to the 15 straight that began in 1969, gives him a string of 17 in a row.

Dave left Baltimore with 181 regular-season wins and seven more in post-season play. Traded to Montreal for the 1975 season, he pitched there without signing a contract. He chose to retire rather than test free agency.

Jack Morris

John Scott Morris

Jack Morris was the winningest pitcher of the 1980s. He was the only pitcher to have won 14 or more each year (including the strike year of 1981) in the decade. Some were critical of his ERA, generally well into the 3's, but Morris pointed out that he was paid to win games and that his contracts did not stipulate whether the victories be shutouts or won by scores like 7-6.

And win he did. Three times he won 20 or more in a season and twice led the AL in wins. He retired after the 1994 season with 254 total victories and 175 complete games. Among the most reliable pitchers in history, he holds the American League record with 515 straight starts and once he went more than 10 seasons missing only one scheduled start. His pitching led three teams – the 1984 Tigers, 1991 Twins, and 1992 Blue Jays – to American League titles and he won two games in both the 1984 and 1991 World Series. He was named MVP of the 1991 Series.

An excellent all-around athlete, he holds the major league career record for putouts by a pitcher (387) and was used often as a pinch runner. When the time comes, it will be interesting to see how much the Hall of Fame voters hold that ERA against him.

Above: *Baltimore Orioles' pitcher Dave McNally winds up against Cleveland 10 May 1974. He has a record three 12-games-or-more winning streaks.*

Opposite top: *McNally was part of the great Orioles pitching staffs in the late 1960s and early 1970s. Pitching for Baltimore from 1962-74, he chalked up four 20-win seasons.*

Opposite bottom: *Jack Morris was a winner, and a reliable winner at that. He holds the AL record with 515 straight starts.*

George 'Wabash George' Mullin

George Joseph Mullin

No less than the great Ty Cobb called the Tigers' George Mullin 'the best pitcher in baseball.' That was in 1909. His 29 wins had led the majors that year, and his .784 winning percentage was the best in the American League. That fall, as the Tigers lost their third consecutive World Series, Mullin was 2-1. Over three Series, he started and completed six games and was never relieved in 58 innings.

Wabash George was the mainstay of Detroit's staff for the first decade of the upstart American League's existence. Five times he won 20 games in a season, and he totalled 197 victories in his first 10 years. How this man has avoided being put in the Hall of Fame is one of the major mysteries of the universe. He pitched for 14 seasons and won 229 games, completed 353 (an amazing 82.5 percent of his starts) and averaged 7.6 innings per game, including relief appearances. And he was one of baseball's greatest hitting pitchers, having compiled an impressive .263 career batting average.

After three-quarters of a century, he still holds more Tiger records than any other pitcher. In fact, very few Hall of Famers can match this great pitcher's career stats.

Don 'Newk' Newcombe

Donald Newcombe

The only player in history to be named Rookie of the Year, Most Valuable Player and Cy Young winner, Don Newcombe was an overpowering presence on the mound for the Brooklyn Dodgers from 1949 through 1956 (minus two years with Uncle Sam).

A huge man (6'4", 220 pounds) whose mean looks belied a mild disposition, he posted a 17-8 record as a rookie in 1949 and led the National League in shutouts with five. For an encore, he won 19 as a sophomore. On the final day of that season, 1950, Newk and another 24-year-old righthander faced each other, each trying for his first 20-win season and the NL pennant. Robin Roberts and the Phillies won it, but the true loser was Dodger manager Burt Shotten, whose failure to pinch-run for lead-footed Cal Abrams ended the season in a close play at the plate.

Don won 20 games per season two of his next three years, and he had become the most feared hitting pitcher in the league, with a career batting average of .271 and 15 homers. Then came *the* season.

In 1956 he scored a league-leading 27 wins and had a .794 winning percentage. He was given the first ever Cy Young Award and was named the National League's MVP. He had only been in the majors six years at this point and was 112-48 (.700). The world was his.

But alcoholism destroyed the big man's career, and he was never the same pitcher again. He hung around for four more years and won a total of 149 games. Recovered now, he again works for the Dodgers, counseling ballplayers with potential drinking problems.

Opposite: *Touted by Ty Cobb in 1909 as 'the best pitcher in baseball,' Detroit's George Mullin led the AL that year with a .784 winning percentage and 29 wins. He was a five-time 20-game winner.*

Right: *6'4", 220 lb. Don 'Newk' Newcombe of the Brooklyn Dodgers. The big man dominated the game in 1956, winning the National League MVP and Cy Young Award with a .794 percentage.*

Hal 'Prince Hal' Newhouser

Harold Newhouser

A heart problem kept Hal Newhouser out of World War II, but it certainly didn't hamper his performance on the mound. For the first five years of his major league career with the Tigers he had problems with control – control of his pitches, his temper and his attitude. At that point, the lefthander had a record of 34-52, with nearly six walks per nine innings. But after having been convinced to try an attitude adjustment for the 1944 season, he became the game's best pitcher. He led all of baseball with 29 wins and 187 strikeouts and was rewarded with the AL MVP award.

That was a hard act to follow, but Prince Hal was up to it. In 1945 he won his second consecutive MVP, the only AL pitcher to receive it twice, and led the league in nearly everything: wins (25), percentage (.735), ERA (1.81), starts, complete games, innings, strikeouts, shutouts.

Despite these two outstanding seasons, many critics were writing him off, crediting his success to the depletion of able-bodied players caused by the war. In 1946, when the boys came home, it was thought that Newhouser would return to being just another pitcher. Talk about clouded crystal balls. That year Hal won 26, with an ERA of 1.94 and 275 Ks.

He followed this with 17, 21, 18 and 15 from 1947 through 1950 to show that he could pitch to anyone at any time. Bursitis, however, had developed in 1949, and his top days were numbered. But when he was sound of body and outlook there was none better: 207 wins will attest to that. His long-overdue election to the Hall of Fame came in 1992.

Bobo 'Buck' Newsom

Norman Louis Newsom

If Louis Newsom had been as good as he thought he was – and told everyone he was – the award we give today for pitching excellence would probably be the Bobo Newsom Award.

But he wasn't quite that good. He pitched 20 seasons over a 25-year period, and during that time he won 211 games. On the other hand, he lost 222. He never pitched three consecutive seasons for one team, and his uniform changed 17 times, counting trades and releases. He spent most of his career on also-ran teams.

Along the way, however, he was a 20-game winner three times, consecutively, and at one time or another he led in nearly every pitching statistic. He was also a 20-game loser on three occasions, and he holds the modern record by leading the league in losses four times.

He had some very good years. His 21 wins in the 1940 season led Detroit to the pennant. But perhaps his greatest year was 1938, when he went 20-16 for the pitiful Browns. Without him, they had a 35-81 (.302) record.

The way he got his soubriquet tells us a lot about him. It seems that Newsom, probably because he was so full of himself, could never remember other people's names. So he took to calling everyone 'Bobo.' Other people – probably half amused and half annoyed – began to retaliate by calling him 'Bobo' as well. Before long it was Newsom's original nickname, 'Buck', that no one could remember.

Opposite: The Tigers' Hal Newhouser.

Right: Bobo Newsom pitched three 20-game losing and three 20-game winning seasons.

Far right: Phil Niekro was signed at age 44 by the Yankees.

Overleaf: Atlanta's Phil Niekro unleashes the first pitch of the 1969 National League playoffs against the New York Mets.

Phil 'Knucksie' Niekro

Philip Henry Niekro

At 25, Phil Niekro was not a particularly young rookie when he first appeared on the major league scene with the Milwaukee Braves in 1964. Up and down for the next few years, he didn't become a permanent member of the team until 1967, after the Braves moved to Atlanta. So in his first full major league season, he was 28 years old. And in only one of seven minor league seasons had he been a starting pitcher.

The year he came to the majors for good he divided his time between starting and relieving and led the majors in ERA at 1.87. He was put into the starting rotation on a full-time basis in 1968, and 20 years later he was still there at the age of 48 – one of only four pitchers left in the majors in 1987 who still relied on the knuckleball. Knucksie ranks in or near the Top Ten in

history in most major categories: Innings, strikeouts, walks, losses, games, starts, runs, hits. And he won 318 games. A good-fielding pitcher, he also won the Gold Glove award five times.

Niekro was a 20-game winner three times, and in 1979 he achieved that pitching rarity of both winning and losing 20 in the same season (21-20). For most of his career an Atlanta Brave, he had the misfortune to toil for some pretty bad teams over the years. From 1977 through 1980 he led the National League in losses, a record.

Phil and his brother Joe, also a knuckleballer, have the most wins (529) of any brother combination in history. The Perry brothers, Jim and Gaylord, are number two with 519.

Al 'The Curveless Wonder' Orth

Albert Lewis Orth

The idea of not allowing the pitcher to bat is not new. It has been proposed frequently at least since the turn of the century. A newspaper editorial around 1910 came out against the idea, giving as one of the reasons, 'Fans would be deprived of seeing such as . . . Al Orth swing the bat.'

Truly a great hitting pitcher, with an average of .273 and 12 homers in the dead-ball era, Orth played every position except catcher in his major league career. He was first a pitcher, however. His nickname told a great deal about his repertoire: 'The Curveless Wonder.'

But he lasted 13 full seasons and parts of two others without a breaking pitch. Control was his forte - 1.8 walks per nine innings.

Orth was a 20-game winner twice, leading the American League with 27 in 1906, when he was playing with the Yankees. (Earlier he had played for the AL in Philadelphia and Washington.) Depending on the reference you prefer to believe, he won at least 202 and possibly as many as 204 games in his career.

After his retirement in 1909, he umpired in the National League for several seasons in the teens.

Right: *Al Orth played every position except catcher during his career. Despite having no curveball, he was a premier control pitcher, averaging 1.8 walks per nine innings.*

Jim Palmer

James Alvin Palmer

A teen-aged girl was once heard to describe Jim Palmer as 'drop-dead gorgeous.' From the sales of his underwear posters many others must agree, but from the mid-1960s on into the 1980s American League batters would not agree.

He first appeared in an Oriole uniform at 19. At 20, in 1966, he won 15 games and became the youngest pitcher ever to throw a World Series shutout. But in 1967 he made the first of many appearances on the Disabled List. From then until the end of his career, early in 1984, he would spend over 300 days on the DL. That's nearly two full seasons.

Ah, but when he was healthy! Even though he was involved in a tempestuous relationship with Earl Weaver, his manager, and neither was ever happy with the other, it didn't affect his pitching performance. He won 20 or more games per season eight times from 1970 through 1978, missing only 1974, when he spent nearly two months on the DL. In 1973, 1975 and 1976 he won the Cy Young Award.

The various injuries and ailments (arm, elbow, shoulder, back) over the years probably prevented him from winning 300 games. But the 268 he did win is certainly nothing to sneeze at.

Right: *Baltimore Orioles' pitcher Jim Palmer had eight 20-game seasons and captured three Cy Young Awards in 1973, 1975 and 1976, despite having suffered injuries several years before.*

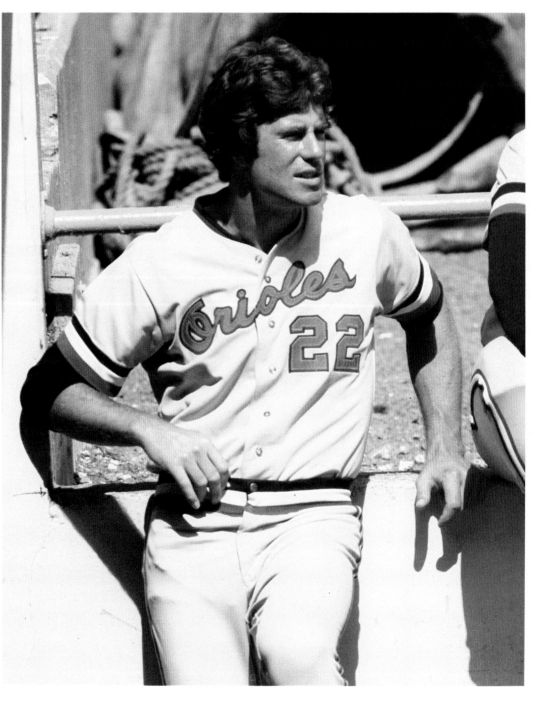

Opposite: *Palmer on the mound for Baltimore. Palmer and other greats such as Dave McNally and Mike Cuellar made up an Oriole pitching staff that led Baltimore to a 1966 four-game sweep of LA in the 1966 World Series and several pennants in the late 1960s and early 1970s.*

Camilo 'Little Potato' Pascual

Camilo Alberto Pascual

Left: *Cuban righthander Camilo Pascual learned the ropes of the pitching trade with the Washington Senators in the 1950s, and later proved to be the mainstay of the ballclub's franchise in Minnesota, leading the American League in strikeouts from 1960-62 and turning in 20-win seasons in 1962 and 1963.*

Opposite: *Southpaw Herb Pennock went to the Yankees from Boston in 1923 for three reserves and cash and turned out to be well worth the trade, having a 162-90 record in 11 seasons in New York and winning five World Series games.*

The Washington Senators of the 1950s were perennial also-rans who generally fought it out with the Browns and/or As for the cellar. Their pitching staff for this decade was manned by some of the most forgetable 'who's who' the game has known. A 20-year-old Cuban, Camilo Pascual was hurried into the majors to try to fill the void that was the Griffith Stadium pitcher's mound.

The young righthander learned and matured while looking up at the rest of the American League. By the time he was 25 he was a .600 pitcher on a .400 team.

Then came the move to Minnesota in 1961, and with it the maturity the Senators had hoped for.

The team suddenly became a factor in the league, and Camilo became a 20-game winner twice and led the league in strikeouts for three straight years. But, unfortunately, at the same time the Twins put it all together in 1965 to win the pennant, Pascual developed arm problems and never regained his peak form.

After five seasons, the immature Pascual had been 28-66 (.298). For the next 10 years Pascual went 142-97 (.594). In his 18 years, he won 174 games.

Herb 'The Knight of Kennet Square' Pennock

Herbert Jefferis Pennock

It appeared that the Boston Red Sox were a minor league affiliate of the New York Yankees in the late teens and early 1920s. The Red Sox were in constant need of money, so to New York went such stars as Babe Ruth (for cash), Carl Mays (for two reserves and cash), Red Ruffing (for a reserve and cash) and, in 1923, Herb Pennock (for three reserves and, you guessed it, cash). With each deal the Yankees got better and the Red Sox got worse.

Pennock had started out with the Athletics, then went to the Red Sox in 1916 and then lost 1918 to World War I. The portsider finally came into his own in 1919, posting a 16-8 mark for the sixth-place Bosox. For the next decade Pennock remained a dominant force among American League pitchers. As a Yankee for 11 seasons, he had a 162-90 (.643) record. As a non-Yankee (also 11 seasons) he had had a 78-72 (.520) ledger. He was a 20-game winner twice in New York, and twice he won 19.

His 5-0 World Series mark was the best on record until his teammate, Lefty Gomez, went him one better in the 1938 Series.

Gaylord Perry

Gaylord Jackson Perry

Left: *Gaylord Perry as a San Diego Padre. He kept his opponents guessing with his suspected doctoring of the ball.*

Above: *Gaylord Perry throwing for the Cleveland Indians. He was a five-time 20-game winner and the only pitcher to win the Cy Young Award in both leagues.*

Opposite top: *Jim Perry of the Minnesota Twins. He earned a Cy Young Award in 1970, making him and his brother Gaylord the only brother tandem to have won the trophy.*

Opposite bottom: *Jim Perry was a hurler for 17 seasons, totaling 215 victories and leading the AL in wins twice.*

It's not unusual for a home team manager to examine a few balls used by a visiting pitcher if he suspects foul play. They are examined carefully for cuts, scuffs, broken stitches and the like. The Boston Red Sox took this a step further in the mid-1970s when Gaylord Perry and the Cleveland Indians came to town: They sent several baseballs used by Perry to a laboratory to try to have them examined for foreign substances.

Throughout his career, Gaylord was accused of doctoring the ball in some manner. Late in his career he was finally caught, but probably as useful as the doctor-ing was the fact that the suspicions kept the opposition guessing, and that gave a psychological advantage to Perry.

To date, he is the only pitcher to win the Cy Young Award in both leagues, and five times he won 20 games. Twice more he won 19. At the end of 22 major league seasons, he had 314 wins, the sixth most losses in history (265), the sixth most strikeouts (3534) and the fifth most innings (5351).

After he retired in 1984 he wrote *Me and the Spitter*. He was elected to the Hall of Fame in 1991.

Jim Perry

James Evan Perry

Gaylord Perry's big brother, Jim, was a top pitcher in his own right, twice leading the American League in victories. They were exactly a decade apart – 18 in 1960 with Cleveland, 24 in 1970 with Minnesota. That latter was his second consecutive 20-win season and earned him the Cy Young Award. Gaylord led the National League that same year with 23 wins. The Perrys remain the only brothers to have won the Cy Young Award.

Although Perry had been an established starter with the Indians in the early 1960s, Twins manager Sam Mele inexplicably used him primarily in relief for several years after he joined the Twins in 1963. When Billy Martin took over the Minnesota reins in 1969, he returned Jim to the rotation, and Perry responded with 74 wins over the next four years, leading the Twinkies to two division titles.

One can only guess how many wins he might have had had he been a starter for those first six years in Minnesota, but he still ended up with 215 for his 17 years of service. Until the Niekro brothers passed them early in 1987, Jim and Gaylord had the most wins of any brother combination – 519.

Deacon Phillippe

Charles Louis Phillippe

In 1897 25-year-old Charles Phillippe decided that playing baseball might be preferable to working for a living. He joined Minneapolis of the Western League, won 21 games the next season, and joined Louisville of the National League in 1899, a 27-year-old rookie.

He won 20 that year (for the first of five times) and was included in the sale of Louisville's chief assets (along with Honus Wagner and eleven others) to Pittsburgh the following season, when Louisville was dropped from the league.

He remained a Pirate the rest of his career, winning 166 games for them before his retirement early in 1911. He won 186 major league games, and might have won 200, but illness cost him half of the 1904 season. In 1908 he appeared in only five games, presumably due to an injury.

Deacon is, and will probably remain, the only pitcher in World Series history to hurl five complete games in one Series. In 1903, in the first Series ever, Boston beat the Pirates, 5 games to 3, as Phillippe went 3-2.

There have been many fine control pitchers over the years, but this man heads the list: 1.25 bases on balls per nine innings over 13 seasons. His exclusion from the Hall of Fame is a mystery.

Billy Pierce

Walter William Pierce

The Chicago White Sox began the 1950s in the second division, 38 games back and eight games out of the cellar. They ended the decade in the World Series. In between they climbed to fourth place, then third place five years in a row, then second place twice. All in all, a good decade for a good team, but faces change as the years pass. The one constant as the Chisox rose from ignominy was their stylish southpaw, Billy Pierce.

Standing 5'10" and weighing only 160 pounds, he gave the appearance of being smaller, but on the mound he was a big man. In 13 years in Chicago he won 20 twice and racked up ERA, strikeout and complete game titles.

The 1961 San Francisco Giants were close to a title, but they were too short on pitching. Following the season, they set out to rectify the situation and sent four players to the White Sox in exchange for Pierce and Don Larsen. Billy, who was now 35 and seemingly past

his peak, responded with a 16-6 mark (in 23 starts) and sparked the Giants to their first West Coast pennant, in 1962.

Pierce called it quits after the 1964 season. He had won 211 games in 18 years.

Eddie 'Gettysburg Eddie' Plank

Edward Stewart Plank

Opposite top: *Deacon Phillipe of the Pittsburgh Pirates is the only pitcher to have pitched five complete games in a World Series (1903).*

Opposite bottom: *Billy Pierce rose from the cellar to the top with the Chicago White Sox, having two 20-win seasons in 13 years at Chicago. In 1962 he helped the San Francisco Giants gain a division title.*

Above: *No lefthander has ever thrown more shutouts than Eddie Plank, and only two southpaws have bettered Plank's career total of 327 wins.*

Left: *Athletics' manager Connie Mack signed Plank directly out of Gettysburg College. Hence the nickname 'Gettysburg Eddie.'*

Hughie Jennings, manager of the powerful Tigers teams of the early 1900s, ridiculed Connie Mack for his frequent signings of college players. (What would 'Eeyah Hughie' say today?) One of these Mack signees was Eddie Plank, who joined the Athletics directly from the campus of Gettysburg College in 1901.

Over the next 14 seasons, Gettysburg Eddie *averaged* over 20 wins a season for the As. Finishing out his 17-year career with, first, St Louis of the short-lived Federal League, and then the Browns, his 327 lifetime wins are the third best total of any southpaw: Only Warren Spahn and Steve Carlton have more. His career percentage was .629, and his lifetime ERA was 2.34. No lefthander ever threw more shutouts – and only four righthanders did – or completed more games.

For much of his career Plank shared mound duties in Philadelphia with Rube Waddell and Chief Bender, and later with Jack Coombs. Their combined arms led the As to six pennants in 10 years, and they dominated the American League. Eddie completed all six of his Series starts, and his Series ERA of 1.32 is the tenth best of any pitcher to appear in the Fall Classic.

The stone-faced Plank was elected to the Baseball Hall of Fame in 1946, and that was certainly an election no one would ever dream of challenging. On my own private pitchers' list I'd rate him the fourth greatest.

Jack Powell

John Joseph Powell

Those ancestral Yankees, the New York Highlanders, tried to win the 1904 American League pennant with a pair of Jacks, but the pot was taken by Boston with four aces: Cy Young, Bill Dinneen, Jesse Tannehill and Norwood Gibson won 87 games among them. The two Jacks, though, established the all-time record for victories by teammates – 64. Jack Chesbro won 41, and Jack Powell added 23.

That was the fourth and last 20-win season for Red Jack Powell, a stocky right-handed spitballer who had the misfortune to spend nearly 10 years with the St Louis Browns. (They were bad even then.) In fact, except for 1904 he only once played on a team that got as high as second place. He is one of two 200-game winners who lost more than they won; Bobo Newsom was the other.

Despite the lack of support he received from his teammates, Powell ranks high on many career lists. And he compiled his stats in only 16 years of playing, whereas most career leaders were active for at least 20 years. His 246 wins put him in the top 30 on the modern victory list, and his ERA was a respectable 2.97. He is one of only six twentieth-century pitchers to have compiled more than 400 complete games. In case any other evidence is required, Ty Cobb considered Powell to be one of the toughest righthanders in the game.

Above: *Jack Powell pitched for the New York Highlanders and the St Louis Browns. He had 246 wins in 16 years of play.*

Opposite: *Dan Quisenberry sends one humming for the Royals.*

Dan 'Quiz' Quisenberry

Daniel Raymond Quisenberry

In 1979 the Kansas City Royals were trying to win their fourth straight American League West Division title, and they were making a good run at it until their pitching went kerphlooey. Ace Dennis Leonard's bad elbow reduced his effectiveness. Veteran relievers Marty Pattin (ankle), Ed Rodriguez (leg) and Steve Mingori (shoulder) were lost for varying amounts of time, and Al Hrabosky, counted on to be the bullpen stopper, was averaging nearly two baserunners of his own per inning, not counting those he inherited.

The Royals were forced to bring up several prospects before their time. Twenty-two-year-old Craig Chamberlain came from Double-A and did well, but his arm went, and so did he, within a year. From AAA came Renie Martin, who would hang around for several years of mediocrity. And finally there was

pseudosubmariner Dan Quisenberry, whose poise and control belied the fact that he had had only a half-season above AA.

His delivery was polished by veteran Kent Tekulve the following spring, and Quiz quickly developed into the premier relief pitcher in the American League, racking up 212 saves in his first six full seasons. Five times he led in that category, and three times he led in games. 1986 was an off year, but in 1987 the touch returned. By mid-1987 he had over 50 wins, all of them as a reliever.

Although hittable (more than a hit per inning for his career), his control was magnificent. His walks-per-nine-inning average of 1.4 is the second best of the live-ball era (minimum 1000 innings).

He retired in 1990 with 244 saves.

Allie 'Superchief' Reynolds

Allie Pierce Reynolds

Allie Reynolds was brought up to the Indians at the end of 1942 to help a pitching staff decimated by the war. He was 27 at the time, and he was coming off 18 wins in Class A. He threw hard, but he was wild. He neverthe-

less became a good wartime pitcher, even though he developed a reputation for not being able to finish.

Not in favor in Cleveland after an 11-15 record in 1946, with 108 walks in 183 innings, Chief was traded to New York. The Big Apple offered several advantages over Cleveland. The biggest, of course, was a batting order that gave Reynolds plenty of runs, but equally important, pitching coach Jim Turner and roommate Ed Lopat taught him that pitching was more than just throwing.

Almost overnight he became the Yankees' ace, and Casey Stengel would spot him against the best the opposition had to offer – Mel Parnell, Bob Lemon, Billy Pierce, Bob Porterfield and the like. In spite of always drawing the tough assignments, Allie won 131 games in his eight Yankee seasons (20 in 1952) and had a winning percentage of .686. In 1951, he became the first American Leaguer to pitch two no-hitters in one season.

A back injury in 1953 led to his retirement after the 1954 season. He had a 182 victories in a little over 12 years, plus seven more (then a record) in World Series competition.

Eppa 'Eppa Jephtha' Rixey

Eppa Rixey

Eppa Rixey never played in the minor leagues, joining the Phillies in 1912 directly from the University of Virginia campus. One of the larger players of his day (he stood 6'5"), he used his height to intimidate National League batters.

The big southpaw had the misfortune to toil for the Phillies and Reds in rather dark times. On five occasions his employers finished in the cellar (twice in Philly), and on four other occasions they were sixth or seventh. He was with the Phillies when they won their only pennant in the first half of this century (1915), but he didn't really blossom as a pitcher until the following season, when he won 22 games, the first of four 20-win seasons for him.

Pat Moran, the Phillies' manager in their pennant season, had become the Reds' manager in 1919, and he urged the team to acquire Rixey. Just prior to the 1921 season the Reds sent starting pitcher Jimmy Ring and regular rightfielder Greasy Neale to the Phillies in exchange for Eppa. It was a solid move. Rixey won an even 100 games for Cincy over the next five seasons, including a league-high 25 in 1922.

Rixey's major league career spanned 21 seasons. During that time he won 266 victories. The figure, impressive enough in itself, was in fact the National League record for a lefty until Warren Spahn came along to break it in the 1960s.

Opposite top: *Allie Reynolds starts his motion on the mound for the New York Yankees in 1951.*

Opposite bottom: *Reynolds became the first hurler in American League history to pitch two no-hitters in a season (1951). He played in six World Series and won seven games, with a .778 percentage.*

Right: *Eppa Rixey, from the University of Virginia, began his career in 1912, playing for Philadelphia and Cincinnati and chalking up 266 victories.*

Robin Roberts

Robin Evan Roberts

From 1950 through 1956 Robin Roberts *averaged* over 319 innings. For six of those years he won over 20 games (19 in the other year), topped by 28 in 1952, the most in the National League since Dizzy Dean had a like number in 1935.

Roberts joined the Phillies early in 1948, after about a third of a season in the minors, and he remained their ace for the next 13 seasons. The Phillies, their 1950 Whiz Kids pennant notwithstanding, were nothing if not mediocre (or worse) for most of this time, but the fireballing righthander, with his outstanding control (1.7 walks per nine innings), still managed to win 234 games for them.

The work load eventually took its toll, and after the horrible (for both Roberts and the Phils) 1961 season, he was sold to the Yankees. It looked as if his career were over when the New Yorkers released him before he made an appearance, but the Orioles picked him up a few weeks later, and he went on to win 42 games for them over the next three-plus seasons. In 1964, Robin teamed with other cast-offs and kids to give the Birds their first serious run at a pennant. They were actually first as late as August, but they finished third, two games back.

Roberts retired after the 1966 season. He had 286 victories and had pitched 305 complete games.

Opposite top: *The Philadelphia Phillies' Robin Roberts.*

Opposite bottom: *Roberts won 234 games during his tenure with the Phillies and later pitched for the Baltimore Orioles.*

Above: *Red Ruffing.*

Right: *Ruffing compiled an incredible Series record, playing on six World Championship Yankee teams and winning seven games (six in a row).*

Red Ruffing

Charles Herbert Ruffing

He was considered by many to be the best hitter of baseball's great pitchers (an argument can be made for others), and were it not for an early mining accident that had cost him four toes, he might have had a good career as an outfielder.

Entering the majors for good in 1925 with the unbelievably bad Red Sox, he had a 39-96 record with them over the next five-plus seasons. (The Bosox finished last each of those years, with an *average* of 49 games out of first place.) In possibly the most one-sided trade in the annals of the game, on 30 May 1930 the Yankees sent reserve outfielder Cedric Durst and $50,000 to Boston for the red-headed righthander. Over the next

13 years, Ruffing gave New York a 216-120 record, including four consecutive 20-victory seasons. He led the Bronx Bombers to seven World Series and six Championships. He won six Series games in a row, and his seven total Series victories is second only to another Yankee great, Whitey Ford.

Thirty-six home runs and a .269 average are testimony to his prowess with the bat. Over the years, he was called upon to pinch hit over 250 times, and he came through with a .254 average.

Red retired with 273 wins. World War II may have cost him a chance at 300, but then perhaps it was his teammates on the Red Sox who were to blame.

Nolan Ryan

Lynn Nolan Ryan

Sometimes it's hard to win. Detractors claim Nolan Ryan is only a .500 pitcher and therefore has no claim to greatness. Actually, his winning percentage was .526, higher than that of the teams for which he played – about .500 – over the years. In fact, half of his years were spent on sub-.500 teams.

The fastest pitcher ever clocked by the sophisticated timing devices we have today (100.8 mph), Ryan holds volumes of records associated with his speed. He retired in 1993 after 27 seasons and his 5714 strikeouts, 2795 walks, and seven no-hitters are records which may never be touched. Other records: most Ks in a season, 383; most seasons at or above 300 Ks, 6; most seasons at or above 200 Ks, 15; most seasons at or above 100 Ks, 24; most consecutive seasons at or above 100 Ks, 23; most Ks per nine innings in a career, 9.55; most seasons leading in walks, 8; most seasons leading in Ks, 11; fewest hits per nine innings in a career, 6.56.

He retired with 324 wins and 61 shutouts. All those figures add up to a Hall of Fame berth the first year he becomes eligible.

Opposite: *Nolan Ryan holds the all-time strikeout record (5714) and no-hit mark (7).*

Below: *Johnny Sain first pitched for the Braves as a reliever in 1942 but soon became a starter, winning 20 or more four times.*

Johnny Sain

John Franklin Sain

'Spahn and Sain and two days of rain.' The battle cry of the 1948 Boston Braves. Probably as good a slogan as baseball ever had, but it was unfair to the rest of the pitching staff. True, Johnny Sain led the National League with 24 wins, and Warren Spahn added 15, but veteran Bill Voiselle won 13, rookie Vern Bickford added 11 and Bobby Hogue, another rookie, had eight, all in relief.

Trivia: Which player had his hometown on the back of his uniform?

Answer: Bill Voiselle wore number 96 and came from the town of Ninety-six, South Carolina.

Sain's 24 wins in 1948 marked the third year in succession he had won 20 or more. He would do it again in 1950, and he won a total of 95 games in his first five years after he returned from the war in 1946. He had pitched for the Braves in 1942 in relief, so he was 28 years old before establishing himself as a front-line starter.

In one of those rare deals which help both teams, Sain was sent to the Yankees in 1951, just before the deadline for Series eligibility, in exchange for minor league pitcher Lew Burdette and cash. Sain, the formidable starter, became Sain the dominant reliever, as he helped the New Yorkers to three World Championships.

Johnny's lifetime win total was only 139 in 11 years, but three years in his mid-20s were spent with Uncle Sam. It's a shame we couldn't have seen more of him.

Tom Seaver, a three-time Cy Young Award winner.

Tom 'Tom Terrific' Seaver

George Thomas Seaver

When Nancy Seaver married collegian Tom, she thought she was marrying a future dentist who happened to be a good baseball player. But dentistry was not to be in their future.

Tom Terrific needed only one season in the minors before he joined the Mets in 1967. This was not a good team: tenth place, 40½ games out of first, eight games out of ninth. Seaver won 16 games and was the only pitcher on the team with more than nine wins or a percentage over .500. He was rewarded by being voted Rookie of the Year.

In time he became *the* Met. His class and demeanor symbolized the team. Four times he won 20-plus for them, and a fifth time, in 1977, was split between the Mets and Reds. Three times he won the Cy Young Award. He stands fourth on the all-time strikeout list, with 3640, and he holds the record for most consecutive seasons of 200 or more (nine).

Seaver was offered the opportunity to return to the Mets in 1987, when injuries plagued their pitching staff. He tried, but in practice it was apparent that he was not the Tom Seaver he needed to be. He could have held them to the contract, but in typical gentlemanly fashion he announced that the end had been reached and retired.

The final tally: 311 wins, 2.86 ERA, 61 shutouts. He became a member of the Hall of Fame in 1992 in a landslide election.

Urban Shocker

Urban James Shocker

The St Louis Browns were basically a disaster as a franchise, but for one brief period in the late teens and early 1920s they made a mild run at respectability. Not coincidentally, Urban Shocker was the ace of their pitching staff during these years.

In 1921 and 1922, the Browns finished third and second, respectively. (The 1922 edition is generally regarded as the best Browns team of all.) These were the middle two of four consecutive 20-win seasons for Shocker.

During the six seasons of life shown by the Browns they had a winning percentage of .514. Shocker's percentage for that same period was .615 (as it was for his career). He accounted for 26 percent of the team's victories. He holds numerous Browns team pitching records, among them most wins in a season (27) and in a career (126 in seven seasons).

Originally a Yankee, he went to the Browns in 1918 and returned to New York in 1925. There he helped the Yankees to pennants in 1926 and 1927 when he won 19 and 18 games. He returned for the 1929 season, but he became ill and died before the season was over. His career shows a 187-117 record.

Urban Shocker, St Louis Browns ace.

Lee Smith

Lee Arthur Smith, Jr

There have been some great relief pitchers in recent years, but the greatest of them all is Lee Smith, a giant (6″6′, 269 pounds) of a man who seemed to reach a plateau of excellence over a decade ago and has stayed there.

The 300-save level was once only a distant dream for a reliever, but Smith, through 1996, has 473 and 500 would appear to be only a whistle-stop on his eventual destination to a total as imposing as Cy Young's 511 wins.

Smith has been named Fireman of the Year four times (three NL, one AL) and holds both the single-season and career save records for the NL. His ten seasons of 30 or more saves are also the record. In the early portion of 1995, he set a new record for consecutive saves while pitching for the California Angels.

Although he averaged nearly 60 games a year for his first 15 seasons, he has never led in that department, yet he had 997 through 1996 and it would seem that only a natural disaster will prevent him from someday topping Hoyt Wilhelm's 1,070.

The California Angels' ace reliever Lee Smith.

Warren Spahn

Warren Edward Spahn

World War II kept Spahnie out of the major leagues until he was 25, but he hung around for another 21 years, nonetheless, and when he finally called it a career he had more victories (363) and more 20-win seasons (13) than any lefthander in history.

From 1947, when he joined the Braves' rotation (in Boston) through 1963 (in Milwaukee), a total of 17 years, Spahn won between 14 and 23 games per season. He *averaged* 20 wins for those 17 years, and he won 23 twice, in 1953 and 1963.

Again for those 17 seasons: innings: 245 to 310; complete games: 16 to 26; strikeouts: 100 or more each season. Eight times he led the National League in wins, nine times in complete games, four times in innings, four times in strikeouts and three times in ERA.

And he could hit: 35 career home runs.

Many careers have lasted as long and many stars have shone brighter. But rarely have the two been so impressively combined. He may not rank in the Top Ten, but he certainly belongs in the top 20.

Above: *The winningest left-handed pitcher in baseball history, Warren Spahn won 20 or more games in a season 13 times. He had 100 or more strikeouts in each of his 17 seasons.*

Left: *Spahn (r) and Milwaukee second baseman Red Schoendienst celebrate after Spahn's two-hit shutout of the Yankees in game four of the 1958 World Series.*

Mel Stottlemyre

Melvin Leon Stottlemyre

From 1918 through 1964 the New York Yankees finished below .500 and out of the first division only once (1925). Five of the next 10 years they were below .500, including, in 1966, the first cellar-dwelling Yankee team since 1912. Mel Stottlemyre joined the Yankees late in the 1964 season, just in time to help boost them into the World Series and then to endure the next 10 years of mediocrity.

During these dismal years when the Yankees were chasing .500, Mel won 20 or more games three times. In a career limited to just over 10 full seasons, he won 165 games and completed 152. His ERA was 2.97, and he hurled 40 shutouts.

As respectability slowly returned to New York in the mid-1970s, it did so without the arm that had kept them afloat for the previous decade. In 1974 Stottlemyre's shoulder gave out and he was forced to call it quits. One of the more intriguing speculations is to try to imagine the kind of record he might have compiled if he had come to the Yankees 10 years earlier.

Mel Stottlemyre of the Yankees.

Bruce Sutter

Howard Bruce Sutter

Above: *Bruce Sutter, split-fingered fastballer.*

Bruce Sutter's career was seemingly over following a dismal 1986 season, but after a year off he bounced back in 1988 to reach the 300 save level, with exactly 300.

In the 1950s and 1960s, Pittsburgh's Roy Face kept National League batters guessing with his amazing fork ball. The pitch was generally considered a novelty and, like the knuckleball, was resorted to by most pitchers only when the zip was gone. A decade later, Sutter began throwing the fork ball's first cousin, the split-fingered fastball. It is no longer considered either a novelty or a last resort.

A relief pitcher from the day he signed his first contract, Bruce never started a professional game. He appeared in 661 major league games and five times led the NL in saves, topped by a then-record 45 in 1984.

During one four-year period with the Chicago Cubs, he won or saved 149 of the team's 304 victories. His 37 saves and six wins in relief earned him the 1979 Cy Young Award in the National League.

Don Sutton

Donald Howard Sutton

The most amazingly consistent pitcher since World War II, Don Sutton won in double figures in 21 of his 23 major league seasons, ending with 324 victories. This was accomplished quietly and efficiently, with no phenomenal, blow-the-opposition-away Cy Young Award-winning seasons.

The Dodgers, both Brooklyn and Los Angeles, over the years have had some great, headline-demanding moundsmen: Dazzy Vance, Burleigh Grimes, Don Newcombe, Sandy Koufax, Don Drysdale, Fernando Valenzuela, and Orel Hershiser. But most of the pitch-

ing records for the franchise, including the big one, 233 wins, belong to Sutton.

Only once was he a 20-game winner, a fact that causes some to discredit his ability, but his career numbers just can't be ignored. He never led in strike-outs in a season, but his 3574 are fifth best of all time and he fanned over 100 batters for 21 consecutive years, second only to Nolan Ryan's 23. His 5280 innings and 58 shutouts are also in the Top Ten. There is little doubt that he will be honored by induction into the Hall of Fame.

Left: *Dodgers pitcher Don Sutton confers with manager Tommy Lasorda and catcher Steve Yeager on the mound.*

Opposite: *A jubilant fan joins Red Sox teammates of fire-baller Luis Tiant after Boston's winning the 1975 World Series opener over the Reds.*

Luis Tiant

Luis Clemente Tiant

The reference books say El Tiante was 41 when they finally tore the uniform off of him in 1982, but there are rumors that he was pitching in his native Cuba in the mid-1950s.

Whichever is true, he joined the Indians in 1964 in mid-season, after posting a 15-1 log with Portland (Pacific Coast League), and proceeded to go 10-4 the rest of the year. His 25 victories topped professional ball.

A block-buster season in 1968, with 21 wins, a league-leading 1.60 ERA and nine shutouts, moved him up among the game's premier pitchers. Then, two years later, a broken shoulder had seemingly ended his career.

But in two more years he won his second ERA title (1.91), and, now with Boston (from 1971 to 1979), he won 20 games three more times, and his brilliant pitching led the Red Sox to a near World Championship in 1975.

'Looie', whatever his age, ended his career with 229 victories, 147 of them coming after he was written off – and definitely after his thirtieth birthday.

Virgil 'Fire' Trucks

Virgil Oliver Trucks

In 1952 the Detroit Tigers finished in the cellar for the first time in their history. They were the last of the original eight American League teams to do so. When they finally did bottom out, they did the job thoroughly. They were 15 games out of seventh and 46 out of first, last in ERA and next to last in batting and fielding. Only four position players appeared in over 100 games, and only one in over 115. That's about as thorough as you can get.

Virgil 'Fire' Trucks was in his eighth full season with the Tigers. He had lost two years to World War II, but otherwise he had been consistently among the ALs top

hurlers. The fact that he had a sore arm in 1950 limiting him to seven appearances, may have cost Detroit the pennant that year: The Tigers lost out by only three games.

But 1952 was disastrous. He won five and lost 19. But his first victory was a no-hitter, and so was his fifth. Thus he became only the third pitcher in history to throw two no-hitters in one season. In between, he pitched a one-hitter. He won all three games by scores of 1-0. Virgil was a 20-game winner only once. He played in major league baseball for 17 seasons, and during that period he had 177 victories.

George 'The Bull' Uhle

George Ernest Uhle

Twenty-year-old George Uhle joined the Cleveland Indians in 1919 with no minor league experience. In his freshman year he proceeded to produce a 10-5 record with a 2.91 ERA. But then he fell victim to the sophomore jinx and failed to contribute appreciably to the Tribe's World Championship effort in 1920. But he bloomed again in 1921 (16-13), and for the better part of the decade of the 1920s he was the ace of the staff.

The origination of the slider is not known. Some say it was created by George Blaeholder, a pitcher of little distinction with the Browns from the mid-1920s through the mid-1930s. This may be true, but Uhle threw a pitch in the early 1920s that his manager, Tris Speaker, described as 'a kind of late-breaking curve that suddenly moves away from a righthanded batter. . . .'

Whether this was, indeed, today's slider that Uhle was throwing is unclear, but whatever it was, it worked. He won an even 200 games, the last 15 after his arm had gone, and he won 20 games three times, twice leading the league (26 in 1923, 27 in 1926).

The Bull may have been the best hitting pitcher. His .288 career average is the highest among pitchers who appeared in 500 games, and his 52 hits in 1923 are the most ever gathered by a pitcher in one season. A frequent pinch-hitter, he led the American League in pinch hits in 1924.

Opposite: *Virgil 'Fire' Trucks in action for the Detroit Tigers in his no-hitter against the Yankees 25 August 1952.*

Right: *George 'The Bull' Uhle completed 32 games for the Cleveland Indians in 1926 and posted a 27-11 record.*

Dazzy Vance

Clarence Arthur Vance

It looked as if Dazzy Vance were going to go down in history as just another good minor league pitcher who didn't have quite enough talent to hang on in the majors. His trials with the Pirates and Yankees in 1915 and 1918 were awful, yielding a record of 0-4 and an ERA of 4.91.

But back in the minors with New Orleans in 1921, he seemed to get it all together, and in 1922 he was purchased by the Dodgers, who had fallen on hard times after winning the National League flag just two years earlier.

The 31-year-old rookie made the most of this opportunity and developed into one of the game's premier hurlers for the next decade. In an unprecedented feat, Vance led the NL in strikeouts for his first seven years. He also won 20 games in a season three times, topped with 28 in 1924. And this was despite pitching for a team that entered the first division only once in the decade. He led in shutouts four times and ERA three times. His outstanding 1924 season earned him MVP honors.

A Dodger for 12 years, he won 190 games for them. His winning percentage as a Dodger was .592. The team's percentage for that period was .499. Dazzy finally retired at 44, with 197 victories.

Above: *Brooklyn Dodger pitcher Dazzy Vance.*

Right: *Vance, the 1924 MVP, led the league that same year in strikeouts (262), ERA, complete games pitched and total wins (28).*

Left: *Vance finished his career with the Cincinnati Reds at the age of 44 in 1935.*

Rube Waddell

George Edward Waddell

Picture, if you will, a pitcher on the mound in the middle of a game. On the street outside a fire engine, sirens blaring, speeds by. The pitcher throws down his glove and races out of the ballpark to follow the truck.

Looking back, it is probably safe to say that Rube Waddell was at least slightly nuts. Athletics manager Connie Mack would not allow him to receive his full pay, doling out a few dollars at a time as Rube needed it. On road trips, it was not unusual for Mack to assign Waddell a baby-sitter, both to make certain he would make it to the ballpark and to try to keep him sober.

But even though the lefty couldn't handle life too well outside the ballpark, he could certainly hold his own between the foul lines. Depending on the source you choose to believe, Rube won either 191, 196 or 205 games in a career that spanned only nine full seasons and parts of four others. For four straight years in the early 1900s he won from 21 to 26 (or 27) games, and for six consecutive years (seven total) he led in strike-outs. In 1904 he whiffed 349 batters, a record that stood for 61 years.

He left the majors in mid-1910 while pitching for the Browns, but he continued to pitch in the Minors until his untimely death just before the start of the 1914 season. He was only 37.

Left: *Rube Waddell may have been a little off his rocker, but that didn't keep him from leading the AL in strikeouts for six consecutive seasons.*

Opposite: *Hall of Famer Ed 'Big Ed' Walsh went in the books to stay in 1908, pitching the most innings ever in a season (464) and compiling 40 wins.*

Ed 'Big Ed' Walsh

Edward Augustine Walsh

In his first nine years in the majors Big Ed Walsh pitched only one season when his club was in the second division. He was, of course, a major reason the Chisox finished so well each year.

Owning a right arm as resilient as any that ever threw a baseball, from 1906 through 1912 Walsh *averaged* 361 innings each year. He holds the modern major league record for innings pitched in a season, with 464 in 1908. That may be *the* one safe record on the books.

But the arm could not go on forever, and in 1913 it gave out. Before it went, however, Walsh accomplished some great feats with it. He won 24 or more games four times, topped by one of the most remarkable feats in baseball history, when, in 1908, he won 40 times.

The spitballer led the American League five times in games, four times in innings, three times in shutouts and twice each in strikeouts and ERA. In fact, his lifetime ERA of 1.82 is the lowest ever recorded. (The runner-up is Addie Joss, at 1.88.)

Big Ed hung on for a few years after the arm went and picked up a few more wins, finally retiring with 195 and a .607 winning percentage. He has been in the Hall of Fame since 1946.

Bucky Walters

William Henry Walters

From 1933 through 1945 the Phillies stank. They were seventh five times and eighth the other eight. They had the unfortunate combination of little pitching, poor hitting and immobile fielding.

Two months into the 1934 season the Phillies bought a third baseman, Bucky Walters, from the Red Sox. He took over as the regular at the hot corner for the remainder of that season and batted .250 with a respectable .410 slugging average. He also appeared in two games as a pitcher.

That winter Johnny Vergez was acquired to play third base, so the hard-throwing Walters tried his hand at pitching, making the career change at 26 years of age. He met with moderate success, considering the cast behind him.

Acquired by the Reds early in 1938 as part of their rebuilding program, he developed into one of the National League's premier pitchers. He won over 20 games three times, topped by 27 in 1939, and he led the league each time. He won 121 games in his first six years as a Redleg. He ended with 198 wins and 160 losses. In a Reds' uniform he was 160-107.

Lon 'The Arkansas Hummingbird' Warneke

Lonnie Warneke

The story goes that in the rural area around Mt Ida, Arkansas, where Lonnie Warneke grew up, there weren't enough kids to form a ball team, so the young Warneke taught himself by reading books on how to play. At 18 he paid his way to a tryout camp and told them he was a first baseman. When asked why, he told them he thought that was where the tall guys played.

In spite of this, he got a contract to pitch for Laurel, in the Cotton States League, but he performed so poorly that he was released. Signed by Alexandria, he got it all together, and by the time he was 21, in 1930, he was pitching for the Cubs.

He won 20 games three times, leading the league in 1932 with 22, and also topping in ERA, with 2.37. The self-taught pitcher won 193 games in 15 seasons. World War II cost him nearly two years at the end of his career, and but for that he might have reached 200.

After retiring as a player, he read another book, *Rules of Baseball*, and became an umpire. He spent seven more years in the National League as one of the most respected arbiters in the game.

Opposite: *Bucky Walters started as a third baseman for the Red Sox but soon became a pitcher. He was acquired by the Reds in 1938. As a Red he was 160-107.*

Below: *Self-made pitcher Lon Warneke of the Chicago Cubs.*

Left: *Warneke led the NL in 1932 with 22 wins and a 2.37 ERA.*

Hoyt Wilhelm

James Hoyt Wilhelm

Hoyt Wilhelm signed a contract with Mooresville, of the Class D North Carolina State League, at the age of 18. It was close to home, and no one else was interested. It was 1942, and he pitched well, but the only one who noticed him was Uncle Sam, who signed him up for three years.

After the war he returned to Mooresville, where he dominated the league, winning 41 games during the next two seasons and striking out nearly 400 batters. Finally, others in professional baseball could no longer ignore the righthander with the fluttering knuckleball. He began moving up the minor league ladder, having successful seasons as a starter at each stop.

Then, in 1952, when Wilhelm was 29, the New York Giants stuck him in their bullpen. Roughly what would be the odds for a 29-year-old rookie having a 21-year career in the majors? That's what happened, and along the way he appeared in 1070 games and won 123 in relief (both records), with an ERA of 2.52.

In 1959, at Baltimore, Paul Richards made Hoyt a starter for the season. He responded with 15 wins and a league-leading 2.19 ERA. And, in a rare start in 1958, he hurled a no-hitter.

Trivia: What player hit a home run in his first major league at bat, a triple in his second and never hit another in 21 years?

Answer: Hoyt Wilhelm.

Above: *Oriole Hoyt Wilhelm preparing for his seventh straight win in 1959.*

Right: *Wilhelm began in the Class D minors and finished with 1070 games in the majors.*

Vic Willis

Victor Gazway Willis

Vic Willis joined the Boston National Leaguers in 1898. He won 24 games, and the Beaneaters led the league. But for the next seven years, his tenure with them, they grew progressively worse, reaching 103 losses in 1905, his final season there.

During these eight years in Beantown, Willis won 20 or more four times, topped by 27, still the franchise record, in both 1899 and 1902. The latter was an especially remarkable year: He completed 45 of 46 starts, hurled 410 innings and struck out 225, all league-leading figures.

As the team worsened over the next three seasons, Willis' record likewise plummeted. He lost 25 in 1904,

Above: *Vic Willis.*　　　　**Opposite:** *Joe Wood.*

and 29, the modern major league record, in 1905. But then the fates smiled; in December of 1905 he was dealt to the Pirates.

He stayed in Pittsburgh for four years, winning, respectively, 22, 22, 23 and 22 games per season, for a total of eight 20-win seasons. He is co-holder of the Pirates' team record for 20-win seasons, and he helped them to the World Championship in 1909.

In a career lasting only 13 years, Willis won 248 games and threw 50 shutouts. His ERA was 2.63.

Joe 'Smokey Joe' Wood

Joe Wood

'Can I throw harder than Joe Wood? Listen, my friend, there's no man alive can throw harder than Smokey Joe Wood.' So spoke Walter Johnson in a 1912 interview.

Wood's 1912 season with the Red Sox was arguably the best ever had by a pitcher. Twenty-two-year-old Smokey Joe led the American League with 34 wins, an .872 winning percentage, 35 complete games (in 38 starts) and 10 shutouts. He pitched the Red Sox to the World Championship with three more victories in the Series. In addition, he batted .290.

That same season saw a new record set for consecutive wins by an AL hurler. Walter Johnson had won 16 in a row early in the season, and later in the year Wood

had reeled off 13 straight. Bosox manager Jake Stahl was dared to pitch Wood against Johnson so the Big Train could stop the challenger's streak himself. In one of the most exciting and promoted games up to that time, Smokey Joe moved up a day in the rotation and won, 1-0. He added two more to equal Johnson's mark.

Wood had won 23 in 1911, and it appeared the Red Sox would be able to ride his right arm for many years, but in 1913 he broke his hand. While still a good pitcher, he was never again the Smokey Joe of 1912. He rounded out his career as a regular in the Cleveland outfield in 1922. All told, he won 116, lost 57 (.671) and had an impressive ERA of 2.03.

Early 'Gus' Wynn

Early Wynn

Stuck with the weak Washington Senators for the decade of the 1940s (minus one and a half years with Uncle Sam), Early Wynn was regarded as a tough and able competitor, but not as a great pitcher.

In eight years with Washington Gus won 72, lost 87, and struck out only 2.7 batters per nine innings. Traded to Cleveland after the 1948 season, he almost immediately became one of the game's top hurlers, winning 20 or more games per season four times for the Tribe and amassing 163 victories in nine years. Swapped to the White Sox for the 1958 season, he won 20 for the fifth time in 1959, winning the Cy Young Award at age 39 and leading the Pale Hose to their first World Series in 40 years.

Early led the league in strikeouts twice, and once he had left the Senators he averaged 5.3 whiffs per game. His reputation as a pitcher who would knock a batter down if he felt it was indicated was well justified. An oft-told story goes like this: Once it was suggested to him that he would knock down his own mother if she batted against him. 'Well,' he replied, 'Mom was an awfully good hitter.'

He was a good batsman himself, knocking out 17 homers. Wynn hurled for a total of 23 seasons, and in that time he won an even 300 games. He has been in the Hall of Fame since 1971.

Cy Young

Denton True Young

In 1956 it was decided to give an award in major league baseball to the outstanding pitcher each season. It is not the Walter Johnson Award or the Christy Mathewson Award or the Award for Good Throwing. It is the Cy Young Award. Very few times has its winner measured up to the standards set by baseball's greatest pitcher.

On some recent lists of the great pitchers Cy Young has not been ranked first. This is simply nonsensical. Where else can you put him?

Other pitchers have pitched as many (22) or more seasons than he did, but none can approach his phenomenal totals. His 511 wins are 95 more than the second best pitcher and 138 more than the third best. He pitched over 1400 innings more than anyone else, he had over 100 more complete games and he walked fewer than 1.5 batters per nine innings for his career.

Pitching in Cleveland and St Louis in the National League and for Boston in the American League, 16 times (14 in a row) he won 20 or more games in a season. Thirteen is the next best total. Five times he topped 30 victories. He hurled three no-hitters. Included in them was the first perfect game of the twentieth century.

Wins are what counts, and Cy has the numbers. The best anyone else can do is come in second.

Opposite: *Early 'Gus' Wynn became a 300-game winner in July 1963.*

Right: *The great Cy Young had 16 20-or-more win seasons.*

THE 100 GREATEST PITCHERS

(BY RANK)

1. Cy Young
2. Walter Johnson
3. Christy Mathewson
4. Eddie Plank
5. Sandy Koufax
6. Grover Cleveland Alexander
7. Addie Joss
8. Lefty Grove
9. Tom Seaver
10. Carl Hubbell
11. Bob Feller
12. Bob Gibson
13. Joe McGinnity
14. Warren Spahn
15. Jim Palmer
16. Hal Newhouser
17. Ted Lyons
18. Dizzy Dean
19. George Mullin
20. Ferguson Jenkins
21. Denny McLain
22. Wilbur Cooper
23. Mordecai Brown
24. Whitey Ford
25. Urban Shocker
26. Steve Carlton
27. Red Faber
28. Juan Marichal
29. Robin Roberts
30. Mel Stottlemyre
31. Vic Willis
32. Jim Bunning
33. Bob Lemon
34. Nolan Ryan

35. Mickey Lolich
36. Red Ruffing
37. Rube Waddell
38. Greg Maddux
39. Wes Ferrell
40. Mel Harder
41. Lefty Gomez
42. Jack Morris
43. Herb Pennock
44. Bobo Newsom
45. Bucky Walters
46. Stan Coveleski
47. Carl Mays
48. Jim Hunter
49. Gaylord Perry
50. Al Orth
51. Chief Bender
52. Jack Powell
53. Paul Derringer
54. Roger Clemens
55. Camilo Pascual
56. Johnny Sain
57. Bert Blyleven
58. Deacon Phillippe
59. Don Drysdale
60. Phil Niekro
61. Ed Walsh
62. Ed Cicotte
63. Don Sutton
64. Jack Chesbro
65. Mike Cuellar
66. George Uhle
67. Luis Tiant
68. Allie Reynolds

69. Dazzy Vance
70. Waite Hoyt
71. Early Wynn
72. Jim Perry
73. Billy Pierce
74. Eppa Rixey
75. George Dauss
76. Hoyt Wilhelm
77. Burleigh Grimes
78. Lee Smith
79. Dutch Leonard
80. Dennis Eckersley
81. Jim Kaat
82. Tommy Bridges
83. Rube Marquard
84. Ray Kremer
85. Dave McNally
86. Sad Sam Jones
87. Tommy John
88. Ed Lopat
89. Murry Dickson
90. Lon Warneke
91. Lindy McDaniel
92. Dan Quisenberry
93. Rollie Fingers
94. Bruce Sutter
95. Don Newcombe
96. Ron Guidry
97. Smokey Joe Wood
98. Goose Gossage
99. Dennis Martinez
100. Lew Burdette

Opposite: *The feats and accomplishments of the legendary Cy Young are an inspiration to all modern-day pitchers.*

INDEX

PHOTO CREDITS

Allsport: J Daniel 58 (bottom); S Dunn 6 (bottom right), 7 (bottom), 57, 91 (bottom); O Greule 23 (top); S Halleran 6 (top); J Jacobsohn 23 (bottom); J Patronite 2-3.
Nancy Hogue: 5 (top left), 7 (top right), 14, 33, 44, 45, 74, 75, 78 (left), 94, 97.
Dwayne Labaacus: 58(top).
Ronald C Modra: 7 (top left), 36, 71 (right), 82, 88, 93 (bottom).
National Baseball Library, Cooperstown, NY: 1, 6 (bottom left), 8 (both), 9, 10 (bottom), 11, 12 (top), 13, 15 (top), 18 (both), 19 (top), 20 (bottom), 21, 22 (bottom), 26, 28 (top), 29 (top), 31, 37, 38 (left), 39, 40, 46, 47, 49, 52, 54, 55, 56, 59, 60, 62, 63 (right), 67 (top), 68, 71 (left), 76, 77, 81 (bottom), 83, 84 (bottom), 85, 87 (right), 92(top), 97, 99 (both), 100, 101, 102, 103 (left), 107, 108, 110.
Reuters/Bettmann: 16(bottom).
UPI/Bettmann Newsphotos: 1, 5 (all four but top left), 10 (top), 12 (bottom), 15 (bottom), 17, 19 (bottom), 20 (top), 22 (top), 23, 24 (both), 27, 28 (bottom), 29 (bottom), 30, 32, 34, 35, 38 (right), 41, 42-3, 48, 50, 51, 53, 61, 63 (left), 64 (both), 65, 66-7, 67 (bottom), 69, 70, 72, 73, 78 (right), 79 (both), 80 (both), 81 (top), 84 (top), 86 (both), 87 (left), 88, 89, 90, 91 (top), 92 (bottom), 93 (top), 95, 98, 103 (right), 104, 104-5, 106, 109.

ACKNOWLEDGEMENTS

The author and publisher would like to thank the following people who helped in the preparation of this book: Mike Rose, who designed it; John Kirk, who edited it; Donna Cornell Muntz, who did the picture research; and Cynthia Klein, who prepared the index.